THE ELEGANT GARDEN

For Helga

THE ELEGANT GARDEN

Architecture and Landscape of the World's Finest Gardens

Johann Kräftner

Levens Hall
Cumbria

CONTENTS

THE GARDEN

A Place of Eternal Life

The garden as a memory of lost paradise is a subject found throughout human history—in religion, poetry, fine arts, and science. The idea of paradise is a projection of wishes and desires that cannot be attained on Earth—and a garden becomes its earthly reflection. The word *paradise* itself relates to the garden and has its origin in the ancient languages of the Middle East, where two similar words, *pairi.daêza* in the East Iranian Avestan language and *pairi-dae'-za* in the Old Persian language of southwest Iran, describe the walled-in garden of the king, where he gathers plants and animals from his empire. Starting in the eleventh century B.C., the Assyrian rulers created similar gardens. A fence, a wall, or a rampart demarcated the Babylonian *paradisu*, which occupied its own realm in an area shielded from the outside world. Ultimately, the Greeks borrowed their term παράδεισος (*parádeisos*) from ancient Asian languages, from which it infiltrated most European languages. The Greeks clearly separated this term from the word τέμενος (*Témenos*), which defined the sacred counterpart: the fenced-in or walled-in holy area where the temples and shrines were located. The places where plants and animals were brought together—where one devoted oneself to contemplation, ritual hunting, or the worship of gods—were conceptually strictly separated from each other.

The paradise garden can be found at the center of all great myths of the Middle East. In the Sumerian-Babylonian Epic of *Gilgamesh* from the twelfth century B.C., this garden is spared from the deluge and thus becomes a place that is safe from destruction. It appears in the Old Testament as the Garden of Eden, which is described in detail in the book of Genesis (2:8). The four Rivers of Paradise—Euphrates, Tigris, Pishon, and Gihon (the latter two never clearly located)—spring from a central source in the middle of the garden: "A river flows out of Eden to water the garden, and from there it divides and becomes four branches" (Genesis 2:10). Almost canonically, this prescribes a continuous motif for many centuries: In many monastery gardens, water springs from a central well, and the streams originating from there divide the garden into four compartments. The role of water as a life-giving element is thus also codified.

The walled-in garden in various shapes and forms can be found as an archetype throughout history: We encounter it in Egyptian murals and papyri, where depictions, which can almost be described as plans, lay out such parks with all their facets in much detail and bring the gardens of this early civilization closer to us. As a general rule, the center held a rectangular water basin or a canal that traversed the garden; both could easily be accessed for ritual washing by means of circumferential stairways. Rows of date palms, vegetable gardens, and flower beds, as well as vineyards and pavilions, were also significant elements. For the wealthy, a garden was the ultimate luxury. Even in ancient times, it showcased the social status and wealth of its owners, and it was unattainable for common people. Since the days of early advanced civilizations, for privileged classes the garden has been an indispensable part of a residence and also an element of comfort and social prestige—amenities and prerogatives that people certainly did not want to lack in the afterlife; they wanted to be able to enjoy them eternally. The vision of one's own garden thus continued in an almost unfiltered manner in images of kingdom come.

Time and again, the terraced layout of the legendary Hanging Gardens of Semiramis set an example for garden design that inspired the imagination and influenced the drafts of notable architects, including Adolf Loos (1870–1933; design of the Grand Hotel Babylon in Nice, 1923), and later became the concept behind many New York variants. The roof gardens of Rockefeller Center in New York (architects Ralph Hancock and A. M. Vanden Hock, 1933–1936) or the facade garden of the Trump Tower (architect Der Scutt, 1983) are examples of this theme in projects dating from the not-too-distant past.

Athens and Rome drew on this type from the Middle East in another manner and combined it with the courtyard house, which became the predominant kind of city residence as well as rural villa during classical antiquity (the peristyle house in Greece; the atrium house in ancient Rome). Friedrich von Gärtner's (1791–1847) *Pompejanum* in Aschaffenburg (1840–1848) and Emmanuel Pontremoli's (1865–1956) *Villa Kerylos* in Beaulieu-sur-Mer on Cap Ferrat (1902–1908)—which is exciting as well because of its exposed topographical location—feature this design. A more recent and significant example, the Getty Villa in Malibu (1974; 1993–1996), by Langdon and Wilson, reintroduced the theme and attempted to harmonize the characteristic features—the peristyle or the atrium—and the garden at the center with the museum's function.

The gardens of Islam were also closely associated with this ancient tradition. As in the Roman house, the walls of the courtyard house were ruggedly forbidding to the outside world here, and they starkly contrasted with the lavishly planted and water-rich green oasis on the inside. The Gardens of the Alhambra in Granada (from 1238 on) and the Spanish, as well as Portuguese gardens that were later created in this tradition, are important testaments to this unique court culture, and many of them have been preserved to this day.

Both strands of tradition from the East come together in a happy synthesis in the paved or planted gardens of monasteries, the paradises, as they were originally described. Early on, the famous monastery plan of St. Gall in Switzerland, which sketches the various forms of garden rooms, codified the parameters of what a garden could look like at the time. This ideal plan, the oldest in existence in the Western world, was probably created between 819 and 836 at Reichenau Monastery for Abbot Gozbert of St. Gall († April 2, shortly after 837), and it graphically presents all open spaces and their design details, which are based on economic order according to the Rule of St. Benedict. A vegetable garden, a medicinal herb garden, and an arboretum planted with fruit trees are depicted next to the cloisters. The latter also served as a cemetery garden.

A monastery that was shaped according to these fundamental ideas and still exists today is the important Italian Benedictine Abbey Praglia at the bottom of the Euganei Hills, close to Padua. Its first building was completed in 1124. Starting in 1480, under the supervision of Tullio Lombardo (1455–1532), the entire complex was redesigned to conform to the Renaissance cannon of perfect form in a virtually ideal manner, and it still exists in this redesigned state. Here, the green *chiostro botanico* of 1480 and the *giardino pensile* of 1490 form an exciting pair of opposites. The previous Romanesque structure of the latter, which is situated one story higher and is made of stone, had been described as *Il Paradiso*; rainwater is collected in it for the purpose of irrigating the lower garden. Another cloister, referred to as *chiostro rustico* (1550–1600), indicates the significance of the economic aspect of such a facility, which for most us is only associated with contemplation. *Ora et labora* (pray and work)—spiritual content and the reality of day-to-day economic management—are present here in a manner that is not only characteristic of a monastic life, but also represents the overall concept of the Renaissance garden in Italy and beyond that Western, and even Islamic, gardens throughout history.

The idea of a demarcated garden continues to appear repeatedly in late medieval and early Renaissance illustrations. *The Golden Age* (1530) by Lucas Cranach the Elder (1475–1553) reflects the worldly and profane side of paradise. Men and women, innocently naked, as well as animals and plants are harmoniously united in a garden surrounded by a brick wall. The rugged world beyond, here symbolized by a wild alpine rock landscape, remains on the outside. One could interpret Stefan Lochner's (1400/10–1451) *Madonna of the Rose Bower* (ca. 1450) as a sacral variant of that painting. This scene is also set in a garden—this time, a heavenly one that is spread out in front of a precious gold background. In the former painting, the focus is on a group of naked figures dancing around a tree of

paradise; and in the latter, the central subject is Mary with baby Jesus on her lap, surrounded by music-making angels.

In *The Garden of Paradise* (ca. 1410/20) by the Master of the Upper Rhine, Mary, with Jesus as a young child lightheartedly plucking an instrument, are also sitting in a walled-in garden with rich vegetation. Courtiers in colorful garments move about in this bucolic ambience, and even an angel is in their midst, attentively listening to the dialogue between two boys. A water basin is among the fixed elements. Motifs from the Middle East and Western medieval times combine into an impressive vision of lost paradise, which lives on in all these small treasures.

A very similar scene, again with exclusively profane content, is shown in a miniature of the love garden from the French poem *Roman de la Rose* (1490/1500). The center here is also a well-arranged garden with an artistically crafted water basin, around which a group of courtiers in colorful clothes is gathered, making music and conversing. This paradise almost turns into a caricature in *The Unicorn in Captivity* of the famous Unicorn Tapestries (1495–1505), in which the legendary mythical creature is held captive in a paradisiacal, but small, fenced-in flower garden with a single tall tree.

Poliphil's famous dream in the book *Hypnerotomachia Poliphili* by Francesco Colonna (1433/34–1527; first Latin edition, 1467) provides us with the first illustrations of gardens during the transition from the Middle Ages to the Renaissance. The last of the woodcut vignettes of the first Italian edition (1499) represents *Poliphil and Polia Sitting with the Nymphs in Front of the Venus Fountain* in a small garden that is clearly demarcated. Another illustration depicts the couple in front of the landscape of the ancient ruins of the Polyandrion, which is also a motif that would soon be found in Renaissance gardens and constitutes an early example of the nostalgia for ruins. This ruin romanticism will play a central role much later—during the second half of the eighteenth and the beginning of the nineteenth century.

The idea of the early garden is characterized by the separation from the outside world, which was probably not merely an imagined threat, but historically actually associated with many dangers. A garden was something that could be wrested from nature, and it therefore required protection. Concomitantly, the garden always remained inaccessible to the public, and mysterious. For this reason, it was the source and origin of myths.

The world of the Renaissance rediscovered this old relationship; beginning with Homer's ελύσιον (*Elysion*), the island world surrounded by Oceanus, far out in the sea off the coast of western Europe, where the Gods' favorite heroes landed when they were given immortality. These Elysian Fields were a paradise on Earth, where the chosen were allowed to live in eternal harmony with nature. However, the Renaissance also discovered another facet of the ideal landscapes of antiquity: Arcadia, which the descriptions of poets had turned into a bucolic, timelessly peaceful cultural landscape, where human beings, flora, and fauna could come together in harmonious unity.

Painters of the Baroque period, such as Claude Lorrain (1600–1682) and Nicolas Poussin (1594–1665), idealized this cohabitation in their work. At this point, however, the opposite of the type of garden we have been discussing appears for the first time: a paradise that, in this case, is not distant and separate from day-to-day living, but rather combines in a bucolic manner the rural everyday world of living and working. This model also has an equivalent in the literature of anti-quity: Virgil's (70–29 B.C.) *Georgica*, an instructional poem in four volumes on the topic of land cultivation, composed in 37–29 B.C., was a source often used later by designers of early landscape gardens. The garden described by Virgil no longer has boundaries—walls or rigid canals that serve to demarcate or organize it—but flows into the surrounding open scenery. This is no longer scary or threatening for humans, but rather a welcoming terrain with which one feels connected. We thus arrive at an entirely different garden model, one that inspires the desire to explore open nature and live in perfect harmony with it.

The transition from the idea of a small, fenced-in paradise to the understanding of a much larger natural expanse had begun quite early, when Petrarch (Francesco Petrarca, 1304–1374), coming from his small house in Arquà, close to Padua (which has a tiny, contemplative courtyard in the front), traveled to southern France and climbed Mount Ventoux—which has an elevation of 6,723 feet above sea level—in the foothills of Provence. Petrarch recorded the adventure in a letter to the humanist Dionigi di Borgo San Sepolcro, and not least because of this document, the poet's historic ascent became one of the key symbols for the triumph over the Middle Ages and the burgeoning of early humanism.

After this, it was a long time before this attitude was commonly understood. We are familiar with the descriptions of the conquest of the Alps, and we know how reluctantly even modest summits were initially climbed; this did not occur until the end of the eighteenth and the beginning of the nineteenth century. Nonetheless, nature increasingly became a friend bent to human will, and reflecting this view, by the middle of the eighteenth century, gardens strived to counter the limitations associated with walls and take possession of a landscape that is visually as unrestricted as possible. Naturally, this freedom also had to be regulated. No English lord wanted to have sheep and cattle in areas of his garden where he had to walk. So an attempt was made to feign endless expanse, to adorn oneself with borrowed plumes. Accordingly, a church steeple with a pointy roof in a village in the distance could quickly mutate into an obelisk as seen from afar; an even vaster park landscape than the one that was actually there could be imagined—for example, in the Wörlitz Garden realm of Saxony-Anhalt. The ruggedly rising mountain ridges behind Edinburgh's Palace of Holyroodhouse, which are covered by bright yellow flora and form the palace's most impressive and farthest backdrop, are also only borrowed and lie far beyond the boundaries of the actual park. For the visitor of

the estates—nowadays owned by the Queen of England—they are a natural part of the scenario; if a vehicle cuts through the picture at the foot of the mountain, it destroys the illusion in a moment.

By tearing down the walls and eliminating all boundaries, a fusion of park and landscape was achieved, and various functions were blended. In the era of the English garden, beauty was combined with functionality; the park and the surrounding agricultural land became an intertwined economic unit that made sense. In terms of content, we are thus not too far removed from the gardens of antiquity, of medieval monasteries, or of the Renaissance, which were the models for this unity, this ecological balance, which substantiated their aesthetics.

If the European garden is a reflection of paradise, a stylization of an imaginary order of the next world that adapts to the various cultural and societal requirements, then the garden of the Far East in China and Japan is a reflection of nature, of the countries' own landscapes in their fascinating manifestations: the mountains and the large rivers, the deserts, and the ocean. These are gardens that respect and glorify nature in all its forms: in the trees that are treated with the same respect and care as would be given to an old person; in the mosses that are cleaned and groomed like a favorite pet; in the stones that have been hauled into these gardens from thousands of miles away and that add the characteristic atmosphere of a picturesque landscape to the garden setting. These are gardens where we can endlessly savor the contrast between stylization and abstraction against the backdrop of perfect nature and where garden and architecture can ultimately enter an intimate and open relationship with a diversity of facets that continues to surprise. In this regard, Far Eastern gardens are virtually counterworlds to the forms of the European garden, and for this reason in particular, they attracted wide interest in the West early on.

In reaction to the strict forms of the Baroque era, shaped by absolutism, and along with the Chinoiserie of the eighteenth century, which already began with Johann Bernhard Fischer von Erlach's *Entwurff Einer Historischen Architectur*, published in its entirety for the first time in 1721, a window opens even in the West for the adventure with nature. A new view of Arcadia becomes the great ideal. The painters initially rediscover it, and subsequently they even provide models for the staging of real nature with their art, such as that of the painter Hubert Robert (1733–1808) in France. The Enlightenment aspiration for freedom, which is behind the movement of landscape gardens, encouraged a quest for knowledge about the gardens of faraway countries. People began systematically to bring home plants from these countries, not only out of an appreciation for their beauty or rarity, but also because they hoped to benefit from them economically.

This new freedom brought with it an unprecedented, impartial approach to architecture and its historically evolved repertoire of shapes, which became evident especially in the imaginative follies (staffages, ornamental buildings) and garden pavilions of the early landscape gardens and continued through the historicism of the second half of the nineteenth century. One of those who utilized the new range of architectural forms was the Slovenian architect Jože Plečnik (1872–1957), who grew up in Vienna. It is seen in his redesign of the Prague Palace Gardens (1920–1935), commissioned by the first president of the Czech Republic, Tomáš Garrigue Masaryk. Later, in an even more concentrated manner, he simultaneously looked back and far ahead in expanding the cemetery of Žale (1938–1940) in his native town of Ljubljana—so much so that he alienated the motifs of ancient architecture. Plečnik's contribution to the history of architecture was not fully understood until the postmodernist period of the late twentieth century.

At the beginning of the twentieth century, cemeteries became a new venue for garden design. In their project for the new Skogskyrkogården (forest cemetery; competition in 1915, start of implementation in 1917) in Stockholm, Erik Gunnar Asplund (1885–1940) and Sigurd Lewerentz (1885–1975) accomplished the same balancing act as Plečnik did before them. With their retrospective take on the Arcadia of the landscape garden, they created a future model for the "gardens of the dead."

Another architect, the Venetian Carlo Scarpa (1906–1978)—one of the most elegant of the twentieth century—reflects on the gardens of Japan for such a project. Scarpa designed the Tomba Brion (1970–1973), a small city of the dead for the Venetian industrialist family Brion in San Vito di Altivole, south of Asolo in the region of the Veneto. On the one hand, he created something like an ancient Temenos, and on the other hand, he borrowed endlessly from the Japanese garden. We can see clearly here how the most creative designers do not necessarily turn to flat, imitative historicism when reflecting on the past but can find entirely new, surprising, contemporary—and thus interesting as well as valid—solutions.

Throughout history, gardens, architecture, and artifacts have been combined in a great variety of ways. It is not easy to determine which one of the conjoined elements is the most important. In the ideal case, no part could exist or be complete without the other. The surrounding landscape gives a building its roots, anchors it to its place, and makes it seem immovable there. In our perception, the tree and the allée are always the primary elements, which are then joined by the architecture or the sculpture. In reality, in most cases the situation is initially the opposite: the house, the sculpture, or other buildings are standing first, and only then are plantings added to them. Who has ever had the idea of building his house in a place where it can be sheltered by an enormous tree? Who has ever built his courtyard around a central tree? It is only in our perception that the sequence is reversed. We then quickly assume that the topos has always been defined by the tree. By implication, the tree, the vegetation, gives the house its immutable position and confers naturalness and imperturbability on it. The monument of the tree and the house together becomes an unyielding topos. The house in a meadow lacks this weight; it appears movable and random, not rooted in its place.

The subject of this book is the interplay and the unity of nature and the works of humankind. We can discover this unity in Scarpa's tombs in San Vito, and we can experience it on the High Line, which was developed between 2004 and 2009 as a park area high above New York City. Here nature was allowed to reclaim lost territory, and a unique new urban space was created with the aid of designers (James Corner of Field Operations;, Elizabeth Diller, Ricardo Scofidio, and Charles Renfro of Diller Scofidio + Renfro; and Piet Oudolf).

Good architecture is able to change, to align itself with various situations, and to adapt. This effect is even more decisive when plants themselves become the material of architecture, as in the case of the bosquets and trellises, the allées and pergolas of the gardens of the high Baroque, which can hardly be surpassed in their seasonal variety. In Japan, the incredible rapture of seasonal colors triggers virtual pilgrimages, with people flocking to those places—Kyoto and Nara in particular—where they can most intensely experience the cherry blossoms in the spring, or the brilliant yellow of the Ginkgo and glowing red of the maple tree in the fall.

Modern sculpture has also rediscovered the reflection of nature. The deliberate permeation of vast landscape areas (for instance, at the Kröller-Müller Museum in Otterloo, the Netherlands) with the simple and masterful contributions of the artists of the twentieth century is at least as exciting as the tension between the white gods carved out of marble before the closed walls of trimmed hedges at Versailles. The interpenetration of interior and exterior rooms in Japanese temple and residential houses follows the same rules as those applied to one of the most beautiful museum buildings of classic modernism, the Kimbell Art Museum (1967–1972) by Louis I. Kahn in Fort Worth, Texas.

Unfortunately, at the present time, many of these carefully woven gossamers are disintegrating; everywhere, entire park landscapes lie dormant. And it is not clear if this is due to laziness, stupidity, indifference, or pure speculation on the part of the people responsible for it. Here, the cultures of the Far East can serve as a mirror for us. In Europe—the origin of the ancient Greek saying: "Honor old age!"—people nowadays pay homage to a cult of eternal youth that strives to conceal and eliminate all traces of old age. In a best-case scenario, we maintain buildings and protect them; however, we do not hesitate to unconditionally cut trees into arbitrary shapes or to mangle them. In Japan, people think in an entirely different manner. The Japanese gardener also cares for the architecture, and he does not shy away from entirely renewing it in a regular ritual rhythm, unvaried, without any compromise. However, he respects the living nature of plants without any reservation; he tends every piece of lawn and, even more, each carpet of moss. One is amazed to see these gardeners working on trees and thinking for several minutes before daring to make a cut. They act according to a presiding concept of their task, and only when a stroke bows to the overall strategy in a meaningful manner will they make the irreversible cut with their admirable tools.

This constant renewal in a context of perpetuity is a fundamentally significant aspect of gardens. Everyone who explores the history of gardens is aware that they are always a place of tremendous change, which on the one hand is inherent in the nature of the matter—a garden must grow from the smallest of plants, and at some point it reaches its biological limit and has to be renewed. On the other hand, gardens are always subject to fashion trends and varied interests. For this reason, hardly any Baroque garden really survived in its original structure; in many cases, the highlights that are much appreciated today are only historicizing reproductions created in much later periods. Hardly any of the large French parks was spared the furor of the French Revolution. In several of his paintings and drawings, Hubert Robert shows the garden of Versailles when it was already in a state of desolation around 1775. In the Liechtenstein Garden in the district of Rossau in Vienna, Giovanni Giuliani's garden sculptures were severely eroded and weathered around the same time—that is, after barely seventy years of standing outdoors—and by then, they no longer conformed to the new ideal of landscape gardens. The garden of Villandry in France, planted with a plethora of vegetables, is an imaginative reproduction. After the Spaniard Joachim Carvallo purchased the park in 1906, he had the existing landscape garden removed and the park restored to its original, geometrically designed condition. Archaeological exploration and a thorough study of treatises from the time of the Renaissance helped to re-create the original fruit garden.

Nowadays, garden care is the order of the day. The original structures of many of the gardens that we admire today were barely any longer discernible thirty years ago and had to be carefully reconstructed. One must not underestimate nature in all its cruelty here; in this area, it definitely rivals the destructiveness of human beings: There have been instances of entire allées, which grew into their majestic appearance over centuries, being destroyed within minutes by cyclonic windstorms. But even Japanese gardens, which are often thousands of years old, have been renewed again and again, solely for the reason that the buildings increased in size, were moved, or simply eliminated by the threat that is still the greatest facing them today: fire. Who would think that the famous Golden Pavilion in Kyoto is the result of a reconstruction in 1955, after it had fallen victim to an arson attack that occurred shortly before?

The constant transformation holds great appeal: No matter how often one experiences a garden, one will hardly ever have the opportunity to experience it in exactly the same way twice. The weather, the quality of the light, the season, and the vegetation play a large role. In this sense, this book strives to continually remind the reader of the fact of changeability: A garden such as Versailles was not only created for a postcard atmosphere with brightly colored flower parterres and clear blue skies. After all, how impressive is the same situation with low, fast-moving cloud banks in the fall or with the boxwood plants in their entirely different coloration during wintertime. How impressive is the orangerie with its unplanted ornaments that create the appearance of a copperplate engraving from the eigh-

teenth century. Those who study gardens know that architecture is something that has to be able to change, because it is merely the work of men and is thus fleeting. The memento mori concealed within this should provoke our thoughts. However, the fact that each autumnal dying is followed by new germination in the spring points in the other direction, toward eternal recurrence. And thus we have arrived where we began: the garden as a memory of lost paradise.

ARCADIA'S FIRST REBIRTH

The Italian Garden

Even in the darkest days of the Middle Ages, after the collapse of ancient Roman civilization, Italy still remained under its cultural influence to a vast extent, although this is not widely acknowledged. The design of the ancient Roman courtyard house, a habitat that was hermetically sealed off from the outside world by means of walls, where all life revolved around a green inner courtyard, certainly had an influence on the layout of the early monasteries. This was codified for the first time in the monastery plan of St. Gall (819–836), which documents several different types of garden, among them the cloister garden, with its pragmatic arrangement into four quadrants around a central fountain. This type also plays an important role in Islamic gardens; Persian silk carpets from the seventeenth century show us exactly this basic pattern. This is the underlying idea of the Italian garden, as well: a garden that possesses a manageable geometrical field or several garden spaces, where a variety of thematic areas are combined to form an overall composition.

The Ten Books on Architecture by the architect and architectural theoretician Leon Battista Alberti (1404–1472) contain the first written instructions for the creation of a garden. They were composed between 1443 and 1452 and printed for the first time in Florence in 1485. Here, Alberti explicitly refers to antique literature, particularly to Pliny the Younger, and writes about evergreen pergolas, the right place for planting buxus plants, and plants whose medicinal benefit should be researched. We can gather many things from Alberti's texts. It becomes clear how he draws from the era of classical antiquity and regards it as a source of inspiration and a model for contemporary creative work. He seamlessly applies the same rules for built and planted architecture. Nature and architecture meld into each other, as can be seen in the example of the grotto, which played an essential role, particularly in the Italian garden of the Renaissance and the Baroque.

Another important publication is the book *Hypnerotomachia Poliphili* by Francesco Colonna (1433–1527), which was published in 1499 in Italian. Colonna cloaks his garden theory in a novel and even renders a plan for a parterre with precise indications for planting. In the fourth book of his architectural treatise of 1537, Sebastiano Serlio (1475–1554) also shows patterns for the planting of such parterre areas.

The first mature statement of this dialogue between architecture and garden is the Belvedere courtyard of the Vatican. Starting in 1503, Donato Bramante (1444–1514) was employed by Pope Julius II to connect the higher-situated Villa Belvedere with the papal palace located at the end of the premises, which slope down almost 1,000 feet. Bramante's design began at the palace with a semicircular theater and continued with a jousting arena set in front of it, bordered by three-storied arcades on both sides, followed by the first terrace, accessible via a wide flight of stairs. Ramps of stairs led to the uppermost terrace, which was cultivated as a parterre, with scenerylike exedra architecture shielding the villa lying behind it. In this arrangement, all the elements that shaped the European garden for the next century and a half were laid down: the terrace, the flights and ramps of stairs, and the exedra.

With the reconstruction of the antique sanctuary of Fortune in Palestrina by Pirro Ligorio (ca. 1510–1583)—who, by the middle of the century, completed the

Belvedere courtyard after Bramante's death—all the antique building forms that will serve as direct models for the design of the Renaissance garden are established.

Arguably the grandest structure that originated in emulation of the Vatican Belvedere courtyard was the sprawling garden of the Villa d'Este in Tivoli, commissioned by Cardinal Ippolito II d'Este (1509–1572). As with the Belvedere courtyard, Pirro Ligorio was the executing architect, and he had implemented the project by 1572. Here as well, large variations in terrain had to be managed. The solution was a complex fabric of smaller garden compartments that were then rejoined into larger complexes by means of intersecting axes. In principal, the garden was divided into two areas: a level part, through which one also accessed the garden, and a steeply ascending part, which nestled against the east corner of the palace building in an L shape. The *giardino degli semplici* formed the center of the level part, an area of the garden that was divided into four symmetrically structured quadrants by a pathway junction covered by pergolas and adorned with a central pavilion. Length- and crosswise pathways again intersected these quadrants. The beds here were planted with medicinal herbs and other useful plants.

The northern part, which slopes directly uphill in front of the palace, is made accessible by means of steep, straight stairways and ramps. At the base is a series of ponds, whose axis continues sharply upward at the north end and is dominated by the powerful prospect of the water organ. Parallel to this runs the Path of Canals, which connects the Fontana di Tivoli and the Fontana di Roma. At the foot of the rock wall of the Fontana di Tivoli, one of the tributaries of the Aniene River arises. This "source" counts among the most significant attractions of the garden, which also include the statue of Tiber in a stone ship, the sculpture of Roma, towering over everything, as well as the Fontana di Roma. They were intended to represent ancient Rome in miniature with its movable elements, which are greatly reduced nowadays.

The other outstanding preserved example of a Renaissance garden in Italy is the garden of the Villa Lante in Bagnaia. It was created shortly after 1566 for Cardinal Giovanni Francesco Gambara (1533–1587), bishop of Viterbo. The architect was Giacomo Barozzi da Vignola (1507–1573), who was able to complete the park around the end of the century. Here, the intention, which was to avoid any display of splendor in the buildings themselves and to direct all attention to the park, is clearly visible. Essentially, the architectural structures are limited to two three-axes pavilions that mark the transition from the flat parterre below, which is lying above the town, and the terraces situated behind it, which are steeply ascending and adorned with waterworks. In the center of the parterre, there is a circular fountain that is complemented by four flanking water pools in a manner that forms a large square expanse of water in the middle. In the upper garden, everything revolves around the theme of water; famous features are the Tavola del Cardinale, with a water channel in its center for the purpose of cooling wine bottles, or the Fontana dei Giganti, which flows into a water stairway in the shape of a crab that has been drawn to a seemingly indefinite length. Here, in a confined space, various small, juxtaposed worlds are woven together. While these worlds continue to surprise, they combine to form a harmonious ensemble that today can hardly be experienced in a single glance, as it once could. Only historic bird's-eye-view engravings can provide a perspective of the overall composition, which is also the case with the Villa d'Este in Tivoli. This marks a major difference from the later French garden, which always attempts to offer its visitors a prolonged view at least across one axis in its seemingly never-ending depth.

Structured slightly differently from these two villas, which follow Roman ideals in Latium, are the Tuscan villas that were mostly shaped by the Medici, with their sophisticated taste; for example, the Villa Castello, which was created by Niccolò di Raffaello di Niccolò dei Pericoli (ca. 1500–1550), called Il Tribolo, in 1538 for Cosimo I de' Medici (1519–1574). Even today, the entire park is still clearly designed in an axial-symmetrical manner; in the middle lies the villa with two small *giardini segreti* at its flanks. Behind the villa is the main parterre, with a water fountain in the center, which is enclosed by a labyrinth of laurel, cypresses, and myrtles. A distinctive feature of the garden is the Orpheus Grotto, which is adorned by life-size animals of bronze and marble conveying the message that just as Orpheus tamed the animals with his song, the Medicis provided for peace and culture. All individual sections of the garden are enclosed by walls that once again make all but impossible the experience of the design in its entirety. Many areas are interspersed with fruit trees, which further impede the view, with the result that here, as elsewhere, the garden can only be appreciated in small units.

In northern Italy, in the Euganean Hills southwest of Padua, the Villa Barbarigo and its garden were created for the Venetian procurator Zuane Francesco Barbarigo in 1669 by Luigi Bernini (1612–1681). Built far into the Baroque period, it is a late example of an Italian garden. Toward the street lies the delicate Portico of the Bath of Diana, which serves as the entrance; behind it, an axis opens up with a fountain and cascades. In the lateral axis, subtle waterworks that leave no visitor dry tell of the sensual joy of the Baroque. The Rabbit Island and a labyrinth are situated along the sides of the main axes, as well as seventy sculptures that today still accompany the visitor, among them an impressive *Chronos*, staged in a clearing in the woods.

In Germany, the Hortus Palatinus—the Garden of the Palatinate—in Heidelberg, was the first and also most important park that followed the model of the Italian garden. Since the garden and the castle were, for the most part, destroyed in the War of the Palatine Succession (1688–1697) and have not been rebuilt, the condition of the garden around 1620 can only be seen from a painting by the Flemish artist Jacques Fouquières, based on an engraving by Matthäus Merian and from the engraving work of Salomon de Caus. The garden was commissioned by Elector Palatine Frederick V (1596–1632), who in 1616 summoned the French engineer and garden architect Salomon de Caus (1576–1626), who lived in England, to Heidelberg for the planning phase. When Frederick was elected King of Bohemia (dubbed the Winter King) in 1619 and moved his residence to Prague, work on the Hortus Palatinus was discontinued.

The garden came into existence at the time when Frederick wanted to modernize the castle and its garden in a manner befitting his social status after his "dream wedding" (in 1613) to Elizabeth Stuart, the daughter of the English King James I. De Caus developed a park with five terraces on four levels, which cleverly utilized the difficult terrain. Here as well, the entire garden was divided into individual parterres that were accentuated by diverse structures. In front of the large grotto, a remarkable portal was erected that is deemed to be one of the most significant structures of the park and in part even survived all the destruction. It was flanked by two obelisks; the arch was decorated with thirteen animal figures. A lion at its center, symbolizing the king of the animals, was also the heraldic animal of Frederick and thus served as an allegorical reference to him.

With this park, Italian garden architecture with all its elements—the combination of art, nature, and technology—made a glamorous entry into Germany. Nature and the work of man united in an earthly paradise that had been unknown until then and that was artistically integrated into the surrounding landscape, yet remained rigidly separated from it. Even more so than in the gardens in Italy, a very high level of stylization and abstraction—and thus contrast to nature—was achieved here.

In Vienna, the garden of the Neugebäude Palace must have been a similar marvel. After the disfiguring remodeling and/or plundering under Maria Theresa, it is still an impressive ruin today. The Neugebäude is considered to be the largest palace of the Renaissance north of the Alps. It was created for Emperor Maximilian II (1527–1576), and construction probably began in the year 1569 on the basis of plans by Jacopo della Strada (1507–1588). In front of the palace, in a lowland area toward the Danube, were an enormous water pool and a parterre with two monumental fountains; behind the palace, on the Wagram, there was another parterre framed by arcades in the middle of a wider arboretum and zoological garden enclosed by walls. With regard to its type, the park is similar to the Kielmannsegg'schen Gärten (Kielmannsegg Gardens) set up for Heinrich Kielmann from Westphalia in Vienna after 1600 or the Blumengarten (Flower Garden) in Kroměříž, Czech Republic, which was created in 1665–1675 according to plans by Filiberto Lucchese (1606–1666) and Giovanni Pietro Tencalla (1629–1702). The palace and garden of Hellbrunn, which were set up starting in 1613 by Prince Archbishop Markus Sittikus of Hohenems (1574–1619) according to the Italian model of a *villa suburbana*, are also worth mentioning.

Of the Italian gardens in France, the garden of the Château de Villandry is to be noted here; it had been completely lost as a Renaissance garden before the Spaniard Joachim Carvallo (1869–1936) purchased the park in 1906 and reconstructed it according to historic drafts, with the aim of reinstating the vegetation that was probably originally there. To this end, the views of the architect Jacques Androuet du Cerceau (1511?–1585/86), who depicted many of the gardens in France—which he had not designed—in his engravings, were of assistance. In Villandry, modeled on the Italian examples, various small-scale theme gardens were created at the time of the transition from the fifteenth to the sixteenth century. Buxus plants and various vegetables were exclusively used for the planting of these gardens, which in their own way combined the concepts of usefulness and beauty that corresponded to the ideals of the Italian Renaissance garden. Today, three-quarters of a century after the completion of its reconstruction, this garden is one of the most unusual and colorful that exist, which proves that because of varied implementation and formation, gardens of the same type can present an entirely different aesthetic appearance. The combination of usefulness and beauty, one of the very central themes of the Italian garden, is reflected hardly anywhere in a more convincing manner than here at Villandry.

Villa Adriana
Tivoli, Italy
Built in 118–138. Summer home and retirement
residence of Emperor Hadrian
Left and below: Teatro Marittimo
Right: Canopus

Pompejanum
Aschaffenburg, Germany
Built in 1840–1848 by Friedrich von
Gärtner for King Ludwig I of Bavaria
Left: Viridarium (Pleasure Garden)
Right: Sommertriclinium
(Summer dining room)
Below: Atrium (Courtyard)

The Getty Villa
Pacific Palisades, California
Built by Denis Kurutz, Matt Randolph, and Amy Korn for
J. Paul Getty. Opened in 1974. Comprehensively restructured
in 1993–2006 by Rodolpho Machado and Jorge Silvetti.

Left: Villa Kerylos
Beaulieu-sur-Mer, France
Built in 1902–1908 by Emmanuel Pontremoli
for the French archaeologist Theodore
Reinach and his wife, Fanny Kann, daughter
of Maximillian Kann and Betty Ephrussi
Left and below right: View into the peristyle
Below left: The small garden in front of the
villa on the cape

Opposite: Villa Medici
Rome, Italy
Built in 1564–1574 by Nanni di Baccio,
Annibale Lippi, and Bartolomeo Ammanati
(collaborated from 1564). Acquired by
Cardinal Ferdinando I de' Medici to display
his collection of antiquities. Copy of the
Flying Mercury, 1900, after the original
created in 1580 by Giambologna (original in
the Bargello Museum, Florence, Italy).

Villa Lante
Bagnaia, Italy
Originally built in 1477 for Cardinal Raffaele Riario. Present-day park was laid out in 1566
by Giacomo Barozzi da Vignola for Cardinal Giovanni Francesco Gambara.

Villa dei Vescovi
Luvigliano di Torreglia, Italy
Built under direction of Alvise Cornaro, according to plans by Giovanni
Maria Falconetto (1535–1542), for Francesco Pisani, Bishop of Padua.
Later alterations by Giulio Romano.

Above and below: Villa della Torre
Fumane, Italy
Built in 1562 by Michele Sanmicheli and Giulio Romano for Giulio della Torre

Above and below: Castello del Cataio
Cataio, Italy
Built in 1570–1578 by Andrea da Valle for Pio Enea I Obizzi. Enlarged in the seventeenth century and in 1803 by the d'Este family (Francesco IV of Modena). After the death of Francesco V of Modena, in the possession of the successor to the Austrian throne, Franz Ferdinand, from 1875.

Opposite: Bernardino Rossi, The Gardens of the Reale Palazzo with the Children of Francesco IV of Modena, ca.1830. Oil on canvas.

Left and below: Villa Cigogna Mozzoni
Bisuschio, Italy
Garden designed at the end of the sixteenth century for
Ascanio Mozzoni and Carlo Cigogna Mozzoni

Right: Villa della Porta Bozzolo
Casalzuigno, Italy
Decisive transformation at the end of the seventeenth
century by Gian Angelo III della Porta, on the occasion
of his marriage to Isabella, daughter of Giorgio
Giulini. Addition of the monumental water complex by
the architect Pellegatta in 1723.

Left: Garden of the Villa Balbiano
Balbiano Ossuccio, Italy
Built at the end of the sixteenth century by Pellegrino Tibaldi for
Cardinal Tolomeo Gallio. Further alterations done in 1637.

Below: Viale del Ercole (Avenue of Hercules) of the Villa d'Este
Cernobbio, Italy
Garden and residence built in 1565–1570 by Pellegrino Tibaldi
for Cardinal Tolomeo Gallio. Further alterations through 1784.

Right: Bagno di Diana (Bath of Diana) in the garden of the
Villa Barbarigo
Valsanzibio, Italy
Built in 1669 for Zuane Francesco Barbarigo. Completion under
his son, Gregorio Barbarigo, after plans of Luigi Bernini. Sculptural
decoration primarily by Enrico Merengo.

Left: Fountains in the garden of the Villa Barbarigo
Valsanzibio, Italy
Built in the eighteenth century

Below: Villa Anagrano Bianchi Michiel
Angarano di Bassano, Italy
Planned in 1548 by Andrea Palladio for Giacomo Angarano. Construction completed before 1713 by Baldassare
Longhena and Domenico Margutti.

Opposite: Frontal view and Nymphaeum of the Villa Barbaro
Maser, Italy
Designed in 1557/1558 by Andrea Palladio and later built for Daniele Barbaro, Patriarch of Aquilea and Ambassador
to the court of Queen Elizabeth I of England, and for his brother Marcantonio Barbaro, Ambassador to the Court of
King Charles IX of France. Architectural decoration and sculpture by Alessandro Vittoria.

Opposite and right above: Villa la Quiete on Lake Como. Stairway to the lake and frontal view.
Tremezzo, Italy
Built in the second half the eighteenth century

Right middle: Villa Carlotta on Lake Como. Parterre descending to the lake.
Tremezzo, Italy
Built in the late seventeenth century. Modernized for Anton Giorgio Clerici in 1747.
Villa and park adapted in the beginning of the nineteenth century for Gian Battista Sommariva.
Acquired in 1843 by Princess Marianne of Nassau, wife of Albert of Prussia. Later passed to her daughter Charlotte
and her daughter's husband. George, Hereditary Prince of Sachsen-Meiningen. At this time the garden was created
with azaleas and rhododendrens.

Right below: Miramare Castle. Parterre opening to the sea.
Miramare in Trieste, Italy
Castle built by Carl Junker for Archduke Ferdinand Maximillian of Austria. Construction began March 1, 1856.
Garden designed by court gardeners Josef Laube and Anton Jelinek.

Below: Villa di Rovero. View of the garden.
San Zenone degli Ezzelini, Italy
Built at the end of the sixteenth century for Cristoforo di Rovero

Left, right, and below: Giardino Giusti
Verona, Italy
Laid out at the end of the sixteenth century for the Giusti family. Expansion and adaptation in the seventeenth and eighteenth centuries.

Opposite: Garden of the Villa Negroni, formerly the Villa Morosini
Vezia, Italy
Villa built in 1800 for Carlo Morosini. Garden laid out in 1910–1920 in the Italian style, with elements typical of the seventeenth century.

Opposite: Villa Duodo. Santuario delle Sette Chiese (Sanctuary of the Seven Churches).
Monselice, Italy
Villa built at the beginning of the seventeenth century, according to plans of Vincenzo Scamozzo for Francesco Duodo. Expanded by Andrea Terali ca. 1740. The garden and its monumental sculpture-crowned exedra date from ca. 1740.

Right and below: Villa Fidelia
Spello, Italy
Laid out at the end of the sixteenth century. Restored at beginning of the eighteenth century by Donna Teresa Pamphili Grillo. Further adaptations in 1805 and 1830.

Sculpture garden of the Villa Trento-Da Schio
Costozza di Longare. Italy
Garden laid out ca. 1700. Sculptures by Orazio Marinali.

Villa della Regina
Turin, Italy
Built in 1615 by Ascanio Vitozzi for Maurizio of Savoy. Adaptation and redesign
of the garden in 1692 by Filippo Juvara and Giovanni Baroni di Tavigliano for
the new owner, Anna d'Orléans, wife of Vittorio Amadeo II.

Giardini pensili *of the palaces on the Strada Nuova*
Genoa, Italy

Above left: Palazzo Rosso
Built in 1671–1677 by Pietro Antonio Corradi for Rodolfo and Giovanni
Francesco Brignole-Sale

Left: Palazzo Bianco
Built in 1530–1540 for Luca Grimaldi. Remodeled in 1714–1716 under
Maria Durazzo Brignole-Sale.

Above right: Palazzo Doria-Tursi
Built in 1565 by Domenico and Giovanni Ponzello for Niccolò Grimaldi

Right: Nymphaeum in the courtyard of the Palazzo Podestà
Genoa, Italy
Built in 1559–1565 for Nicolosio Lomellini. In the seventeenth century,
property of the Centurione and Pallavicini families and of Andrea Podestà.
Nymphaeum of Domenico Parodi dates from the first half of the
eighteenth century.

Fountain in the garden of the Palazzo del Principe (Villa of Andrea Doria)
Genoa, Italy
Constructed in 1529 by major artists such as Perino del Vaga for Andrea Doria.
Later property of the Doria Pamphili family.
Right: Taddeo Carlone. Fountain of Neptune. Before 1700.
Below: Giovanni Angelo Montorsoli. Fountain of the Satyr. After 1547.

Villa Torrigiani di Camigliano
Camigliano-Lucca, Italy
Restored in 1636 by André Le Nôtre for Nicolao
Santini, Ambassador in Paris of the Republic
of Lucca

48

La Villa Reale di Marlia
Lucca, Italy
Baroque garden from the seventeenth century at the Villa Orsetti (acquired by Livieri and Lelio Orsetti in 1651). Green Theater (1652), Camellia Promenade, water basin, Grotto of Pan. Largely transformed in 1806 into an English garden by Elisa Baciocchi, sister of Napoleon Bonaparte and Regent of Lucca.

Villa d'Este
Tivoli, Italy
Built in 1560 by Pirro Ligorio and Alberto Galvani for Cardinal Ippolito II d'Este
Opposite: (left) Fountain of Neptune with a water organ at the end of the Fish Pond; (above right) View of the Fish Pond; (middle right) Oval Fountain with a statue of the river Aniene. In the background, Venus Victrix and Lupa Romana; (below right) Promenade of the Hundred Fountains
Below left: Roman ship as a symbol of Tiberina Island in the Rometta fountain
Below right: Water organ

Villa del Balbianello
Lenno on Lake Como, Italy
Villa built in the early seventeenth century. Large-scale renovation after changes of ownership at the end of the eighteenth century and in the nineteenth and twentieth centuries. Garden laid out primarily after 1787 during construction of park for Cardinal Angelo Maria Durini. The primary features of the garden are the climbing figs (Ficus repens) that cover pillars and walls and the monumental holm oak tree (Quercus Ilex Leccio) trimmed into the form of a half sphere.

Left: Hortus Palatinus (Garden of the Palatinate)
Heidelberg, Germany
Garden laid out in 1616 by Salomon de Caus. Oil painting by
Jacques Fouquières, 1620.

Below: Der Kielmännische Garten (Kielmann Garden) near Vienna,
by Wien
Vienna-Landstrasse, Austria
Laid out for Heinrich Kielmann (1568–1659). Engraving by
Matthäus Merian, 1649.

Right: Schloss Moritzburg
Moritzburg-Dresden, Germany
Castle constructed upon earlier building. Restored in 1723–1733
by Matthäus Daniel Poppelmann for August the Strong. Unfinished
garden reconstructed in the twentieth century.

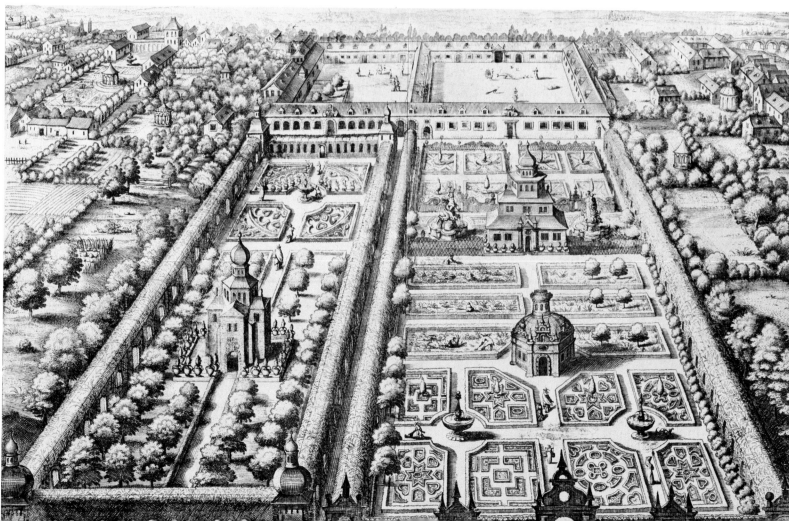

Left and below: Belvedere of Queen Anna in the Royal Garden of the Prague Castle
Prague, Czech Republic
Built by Emperor Ferdinand I of Hapsburg for his consort, Queen Anna of Bohemia and Hungary. Begun in 1538 by the Genoese architect Paolo della Stella and completed in 1556–1564 by Bonifaz Wolmut.

Right: Garden of Palais Waldstein (Waldstein Palace)
Prague-Mala Strana, Czech Republic
Built in 1623–1630 by Giovanni Pieroni and Andrea Spezza for Albrecht Wenzel Eusebius von Waldstein. Sculptural decoration of 1624–1627 by Adrian de Vries (presently copies).

Opposite: Schloss Trója (Trója Castle)
Prague, Czech Republic
Initial design by Giovanni Domenico Orsi de Orsini for Count Wenzel Adalbert von
Sternberg. Construction completed in 1679–1685 by Jean Baptist Mathey. Original
Baroque garden remodeled in the nineteenth century.

Below and right: Vrtborská zahrada (Vrtba Garden)
Prague-Mala Strana, Czech Republic
Constructed in 1715–1720, according to a design by František Maximilián Kanka for
Jan Josef Vrtba. Laid out behind the family palace on the slope of the Laurenziberg.
Sculptural decoration by Matyás Bernard Braun.

Montacute House
Montacute/Yeovil, England
Built after 1598 by William Arnold for
Sir Edward Phelips. Garden laid out by
the gardener Pridham for Ellen Phelips.
Garden restored between 1840 and 1911.

Opposite, above left: Garden bench in the
Huntington Botanical Gardens
San Marino, California
First quarter of the twentieth century

Opposite, above right: Garden bench at
Blickling Hall
Blickling, England
Nineteenth century

Opposite below: Garden bench at Wilton House
Wilton, England
Nineteenth century

Below: Kew Palace (Dutch House)
Kew/Richmond, England
Built in 1631 for the Dutch merchant Samuel Fortrey.
Royal residence since 1728. Queen's garden laid out
in the 1960s.

Blenheim Palace
Woodstock, England
Palace built in 1704 by Sir John Vanbrugh and completed by Nicholas Hawksmoor for John Churchill, first Duke of Marlborough.
English garden restored in 1764 by Capability Brown. Formal gardens restored in 1920 in the style of the seventeenth century by Achille Duchêne.

Jardim do Palácio Nacional de Queluz
Queluz-Lisbon, Portugal
Built for Dom Pedro III. Construction of the chapel wing, throne room, and concert hall in 1747–1758 by Mateus Vicente de Oliveira. Remodeling of the throne room and concert hall in 1760–1786 by Jean-Baptiste Robillon. Construction of the Dona Maria Pavilion in 1786–1792 by Manuel Caetano de Sousa.

Left: Water basin in the form of an irregular scallop shell (Rocaille; Lago des Conchas)

Below left: Labyrinth garden in place of the original labyrinth. Beginnning of the twentieth century.

Below: View of the Malta Garden from the throne room

Opposite: View of the wing with the throne room and the concert hall from the ceremonial hall. The Malta Garden in the foreground.

Jardim do Casa de Mateus
Vila Real, Portugal
Built as a residence in 1739–1743 by Nicolau Nasoni for António José
Botelho Mourão, third Morgado de Mateus. Garden laid out in the second
half of the eighteenth century for D. Luís António de Sousa Botelho
Mourão and his wife, D. Leonor Ana Luísa José de Portugal. Remodeled
in the 1930s and 1940s and decisively altered.

*Right and far right: Bom Jesus de Monte
Braga, Portugal
Begun in 1722 for the archbishop of
Braga, Rodrigo de Moura Telles. With its
chapels, the stairway symbolizes the Way of
the Cross, the five senses, and the cardinal
virtues: Love, Hope, and Charity.*

*Below: Parque Nacional do Buçaco
Mata do Buçaco, Portugal
Palace erected in 1887 as a summer
residence for King Carlos I. Constructed
around several medieval abbeys by the
Italian theater architect Luigi Manini.
Gardens in the English and Italian styles
were laid out surrounding the palace and
the ruins of the abbeys.*

Left: Château d'Azay-le-Rideau
Azay-le-Rideau, France
Built in 1516–1526 for Gilles Berthelot

Left and right: Château de Chenonceau
Chenonceau, France
Built in 1515–1521 for Thomas Bohier. Construction
of the extensive gardens and the arched bridge wing
over the Loire River after 1551–1555 by Philibert de
l'Orme and Jacques Androuet du Cerceau for Diane
de Poitiers, mistress of King Henry II of France.
After 1560, the property of Caterina de' Medici.
Restoration of the garden around 1900 by Achille
and Henri Duchêne.

Garden of the Château de Villandry
Villandry, France
Original castle and garden completed in 1536 for Jean le Breton, finance minister for King Francis I. English landscape garden laid out in the nineteenth century. Between 1906 and 1924, reconstructed by the new owner, Joachim Carvallo-Adelmani, in the style of a Renaissance garden, following engravings by Jacques Androuet du Cerceau.

ORDERED NATURE

The French Garden

Nothing symbolized the culture of Baroque life better than the French garden at its apogee, and Versailles—the castle and gardens of the French kings—was its embodiment. During the reigns of Louis XIV (1638–1715), Louis XV (1710–1774), and Louis XVI (1754–1793), Versailles became the epitome of expansiveness, splendor—and, ultimately, wastefulness. In the last phase of its construction, Versailles was an amazing fabric of diverse independent gardens and spaces, of water axes and avenues; it was an undertaking that had constantly changed in the course of a century. No sooner was an aspect completed than it was replaced by something even more magnificent. Versailles is comparable to a city filled with urban lifelines, with streets and public squares that connect and structure the entire organism.

Throughout Europe it was considered a great status symbol to possess a garden of comparable splendor. The Habsburgs attempted to compete with Versailles through the construction of Schönbrunn Palace, Peter the Great (1672–1725) by building Peterhof Palace on the shores of the Baltic Sea, and even lesser provincial princes tried to emulate its stature. Europe still manifests the results of their efforts, even though the next generation ruthlessly eradicated most of the earlier gardens in the course of embracing a new ideal, the landscape garden.

The genesis of the French garden is particularly associated with two great names: André Le Nôtre (1613–1700) and King Louis XIV, who together were responsible for the largest and most important of the gardens. Their point of departure was unquestionably the Renaissance examples that had come into being in Italy. Striving for grandeur, they took the many small, creative, and practical areas of such a garden, and the many individual buildings that together formed the complete composition, and molded them into an overriding uniformity. In the center stands a mighty palace from which all paths and axes radiate outward or, vice versa, to which all paths lead. Everything else is subordinated to one single view, facing the castle, ideally in an elevated position, with pools, canals, and *parterres de broderie* spreading out into infinity. These are bordered by bosquets and trellises that strengthen the impression of scenic depth by the way they structure the space and that in themselves contain complex spatial diversity and topological surprises.

Le Nôtre's fame as a landscape and garden designer began immediately with his first great creation, the garden at Vaux-le-Vicomte that he designed for Nicolas Fouquet (1615–1680), who, from 1653 and onward, was responsible for the financial administration of the kingdom. Despite many losses, Vaux is still considered to be one of the most magnificent Baroque gardens of France. Even during this first creation, one corollary of such projects became evident, namely the high level of expenditure that was necessary for their realization. Understanding this, Fouquet had set aside resources to cover the costs in a timely manner. Whether it was wise for him to act publicly in such a regal manner, however, was a question that he seems not to have considered.

Fouquet engaged the best talent available for the buildings and grounds: the architect Louis Le Vau (1612–1670), the painter Charles Le Brun (1619–1690), and the young André Le Nôtre. Work began in 1656, and the garden was dedicated on August 17, 1661, in the presence of King Louis XIV, the Queen Mother, and the entire court. It was a celebration the likes of which even the king had never experienced. From the cuisine to the water displays and fireworks in the garden, Fouquet did everything possible to impress his employer. King Louis quickly realized where Fouquet had obtained his money—it had been withheld from the royal coffers. Shortly after returning to his palace, Louis had his superintendent of finance thrown into prison, and Fouquet remained there for the rest of his life. Fouquet's endeavor failed, but the king adopted his artistic aspirations. He robbed Vaux-le-Vicomte of all its portable works of art and employed them, as he did the three artists, in his own project: the construction of the palace park at Versailles. Vaux-le-Vicomte fell into ruin until it was acquired in 1875 by a French captain of industry, who attempted to restore it. It remains a far cry from the original, however, due to the costs that would have been involved in a careful restoration of delicate details. It is from the engravings of Israël Silvestre (1621–1691) that we can obtain the best idea of the vastness of this garden, with the clear axis of its *parterre de broderie* emanating from the castle and stretching out seemingly to infinity. Le Nôtre invented nothing new in the realization of this revolutionary project: the themes of the canal, the pond, the fountain, the water display, the grotto, the avenue, the bosquet, the flower parterre, and *parterre de broderie* already existed in Italian, French, and Dutch garden architecture. What was new was the quality of expansiveness and a seeming transparency that actually masked many surprises.

At Versailles the king went even further; not all at once, but rather in many phases. The result was a total work of art in which many generations of creation, destruction, and reconstruction played a part, and that even today is overwhelmingly impressive. In the critical design phase, the decisive roles were those of the architect Jules Hardouin-Mansart (1646–1708) and Le Nôtre. Le Nôtre designed a garden that was quite visionary. Today it appears in perfect relationship to the gigantic dimensions of the palace. Yet, at the time that the garden was designed, the palace could not hope to compete with it, for no one initially imagined the palace in its present size. Some "instructions for use" written by Louis XIV himself illustrate how important the gardens were to the king as a means of impressing visitors. In the *Manière de montrer les Jardins de Versailles* (*The Way to Show the Gardens of Versailles*), he leads the visitor through his dream of antiquity. The garden evokes this dream with a sculptural program on related themes. Various commissions to depict the scenario in paintings and engravings may serve as an indication of how ephemeral the king considered his creation to be. Twenty-four oil paintings were produced with garden vistas, populated by creatures that had nothing in common with normal visitors: gods come to life in order to document artistically the fame of this creation for all eternity.

As an alternative world to this bombastic garden, the king caused the Trianon de Porcelaine, intended for his mistress, the Marquise de Montepan (1641–1707), to be built from 1670 to 1672, according to plans by Louis Le Veau. This delicate, clearly defined building, adorned with precious glittering faience plates, was already pulled down in 1687, however. The official reason given for its destruction was dilapidation; the probable reason was the king's new mistress, Madame de Maintenon (1635–1719), whom he wanted to honor with an even more elegant and somewhat larger château on the same site. The result was the Trianon de Marbre, begun in 1687 and later known as the Grand Trianon. The house became habitable in 1688 and was furnished with a garden organized to perfection. The relationship of the house to the garden is very refined. Immediately upon entering the house, one enjoys a view through the open peristyle to the expansive flower parterre, completely altered in its modern incarnation. All flowers were set out in pots so that they could be quickly replaced. In a letter in 1694 to the Swedish architect Nicodemus Tessin, Le Nôtre wrote that no one would ever see a withered leaf or a flower that was not in bloom in the Trianon. This realm was dedicated to Flora, and a ballet called *The Palace of Flora* was performed here in 1689. Guests were surrounded by a frenzy of scent and color. Despite its monumentality and grandeur, it was a garden that was accessible in the modern sense of the word, one that a person could enter by simply passing through a French window. This castle complex, which represented a reduction of royal claims of representation, was complemented by Louis XV's construction of the Petit Trianon. The Petit Trianon was built from 1762 to 1768 for the royal mistress, Madame Pompadour (1721–1764), by the architect Anges-Jacques Gabriel (1698–1782). Later on, Queen Marie Antoinette (1755–1793) also dearly loved this architectural jewel, whose garden served as the birthplace of a bucolic country life at the royal court.

In the year 1709, after the death of Le Nôtre, a book titled *La Théorie et la Pratique du Jardinage* (*The Theory and Practice of Gardening*) was published in Paris, enjoying brilliant success and appearing in numerous editions and languages. Its author was the scholar Antoine-Joseph Dezallier d'Argenville (1680–1765), who was only an amateur gardener. His engravings displayed the entire repertoire of design elements for a Baroque garden. In his work, chiefly responsible for the dissemination of French design patterns, the author establishes four basic rules at the beginning: 1. Nature takes precedence over art, 2. A garden must not be made dark or dreary by too many shady elements, 3. A garden must not reveal its beauty all at once, and 4. A garden must always appear larger than it really is.

Dezallier d'Argenville also provided a large number of engravings that illustrated designs for parterres, the planting of garden beds and borders, avenues and hedges, bosquets, bowling greens, arbors, garden sculptures, terraces, and stairways, as well as fountains, lakes, and ponds. These engravings displayed in minute detail the most basic elements of a French garden and made it all the easier (although no less expensive) for the lover of garden art to approach the ideal that the author had established.

The "Austrian Versailles" at Schönbrunn, the summer palace of the Austrian imperial house and the most ambitious attempt to rival Versailles, showed just how difficult the realization of such a competitive project could be. The engravings of Johann Bernhard Fischer von Erlach (1656–1723) represent the first, incredibly ambitious design. In 1688, in an initial grandiose scheme for Emperor Leopold I (1640–1705), Fischer proposed positioning the palace high on the hill where the Gloriette would later stand. He envisioned the palace complex, descending by a truly gigantic series of terraces—impractical if not impossible to build—to the valley of the Vienna River. Fischer transformed the example of Versailles through far more severe, rigid architectonic forms that in their sculptural quality are far removed from merely decorative excesses. All that can be said concerning the second design, the one that was carried out, is that it was actually capable of realization.

The soaring artistic aspirations of the genius, however, were brought back to earth. Now the great courtyard and the palace itself stood below in the valley. Behind the palace, the parterre extended upward to the hill where the crowning Gloriette would be built in 1775, during the reign of Maria Theresa (1717–1780). The Frenchman Jean Trehet (1654–1740) was the first gardener of Schönbrunn and was later given the responsibility of carrying out other major projects. Along with the imperial gardens at the Augarten and at the imperial summer residence, Favorita auf der Wieden, he also designed the monumental garden in the Rossau for Johann Adam Andreas I, Prince of Liechtenstein. The garden craze had taken hold of the high nobility of Vienna. All the great houses possessed not just one but several gardens. This was the case not only in Vienna, but also at the vast country estates in Hungary, Moravia, and Bohemia, where the centers of the nobility's vital interests were really located.

What was good in Vienna was also valid in many other European centers. The most important courts in Germany provided their palaces with similar parks and gardens: the splendid garden of Nymphenburg Palace still exists in Munich, as do the Court Gardens of the Residence in Würzburg. In Karlsruhe and Mannheim, even the design of the cities was subject to a master plan. The garden of Schwetzingen Castle should be mentioned, as well as that of Charlottenburg Palace in Berlin. In northern Germany, the garden of Herrenhausen in Hannover is remarkable. Despite long years of neglect, particularly during the nineteenth century, many of these gardens can be experienced today in their original form, even if they have not (yet) returned to their complete splendor.

The most important Dutch garden, that of Het Loo Palace, also followed the model valid throughout Europe. The buildings and grounds were created by Jacob Roman and Daniel Marot for Prince William III of Orange (1650–1702), stadtholder of the Dutch Republic, who became King of England in 1689. The garden, in ruins by 1800, was reconstructed in all its essential elements, beginning in 1978.

The work of reconstruction was often made possible by valuable contemporary engravings that, while testifying to the vanity of the owners, in many cases bring us closer to the vanished gardens. Particular mention should be made of the books of panoramic views published in Augsburg by Salomon Kleiner. They provide vivid images of many gardens and are precise down to the last detail. Kleiner included most of the gardens of Vienna, but also the Schönborn castles of southern Germany. One should also note the lavish panoramas of the Venetian artist Bernardo Bellotto, who traveled across all of Europe during the middle of the eighteenth century and captured at their height the most important French gardens of Vienna, Munich, Dresden, and Warsaw. He depicted them at a point in time when they "had fully matured," so to speak, and were about to become passé, doomed to vanish before the new fashion of the English landscape garden.

Château de Versailles
Versailles, France
Originally constructed as a hunting lodge by Philibert
Le Roy for King Louis XIII. Expanded in several stages
beginning in 1661 by Louis Le Vau, François d'Orbay,
Jules Hardouin-Mansart, and Robert de Cotte for
Louis XIV. Further alterations under King Louis XV and
King Louis XVI.
Original master plan for the gardens by André Le Nôtre.

Left: View of the Parterre de Midi

Below: View of the palace and the orangerie. Oil
painting by J.B. Martin (attributed), ca. 1700.

Right: View of the Bassin d'Apollon on the Grand Canal

Château de Versailles
Versailles, France
Built in the second half of the seventeenth century by André Le Nôtre
Below top: View of the Bassin du Dragon; the Allée d'Eau on the left
Below bottom: Jean-Baptiste Tuby. Bassin d'Apollon, 1668–1679.
Right: The Brothers Marsy. The Fontaine du Dragon, 1667.
Reengineered by Tony Noël, 1889

Parterre de l'Orangerie in the Château de Versailles
Versailles, France
The original modest orangerie built in 1663 by Louis Le Vau was replaced between
1684 and 1686 by the monumental edifice of Jules Hardouin-Mansart.

Château de Versailles. Bosquets of the Jardin Française lining the Pavillon Française, in front of the Petit Trianon.
Versailles, France
Built in 1750, and rebuilt between 1762 and 1766 by Anges-Jacques Gabriel for King Louis XV and his mistress,
Madame de Pompadour

Three bosquets from the garden of Versailles of King Louis XIV

Left: Copperplate engravings after Jacques Rigaud: Les Maisons Royale de France, published in 1730; (above) View of the Bains d'Apollon; (middle) View of the Obelisque; (below)View of the Salle de Bal

Three of the bosquets of the garden of Versailles of King Louis XIV in their present condition.

Above: Bosquet de la Colonnade. Created in 1685 by Jules Hardouin-Mansart in place of the Bosquet des Sources created in 1679 by André Le Nôtre.

Below: Bosquet de la Salle de Bal. Created in 1680–1683 by André Le Nôtre.

Opposite: Bosquet de l'Encelade. The Half-Buried Giant Encelade, Spouting Fire and Water, Struggling with Death was created in 1675–1677 from designs by Charles Le Brun and André Le Nôtre as a gilded lead sculpture by Gaspard Marsy. The original trellises (1706) designed by Jules Hardouin-Mansart were removed and then restored at the end of the twentieth century.

Palace Park of Schönbrunn
Vienna-Hietzing, Austria
Commission for first palace construction project given to Johann Bernhard
Fischer von Erlach by Emperor Leopold I in 1688. Realization of project,
according to second, reduced design from 1696. First garden laid out in
1695 by Jean Trehet.

Right: Beautification project for the Schönbrunner Berg (Schönbrunn Hill)
with an early variant design for the Gloriette and suggestions for furnishing
the garden with sculptures. Watercolor probably painted by Carl Schütz after
a sketch by Johann Ferdinad Hetzendorf von Hohenberg, 1772.

Below: View through the Tiergartenallee to the palace

Opposite: The Fächer (The Fan) in the bosquet area

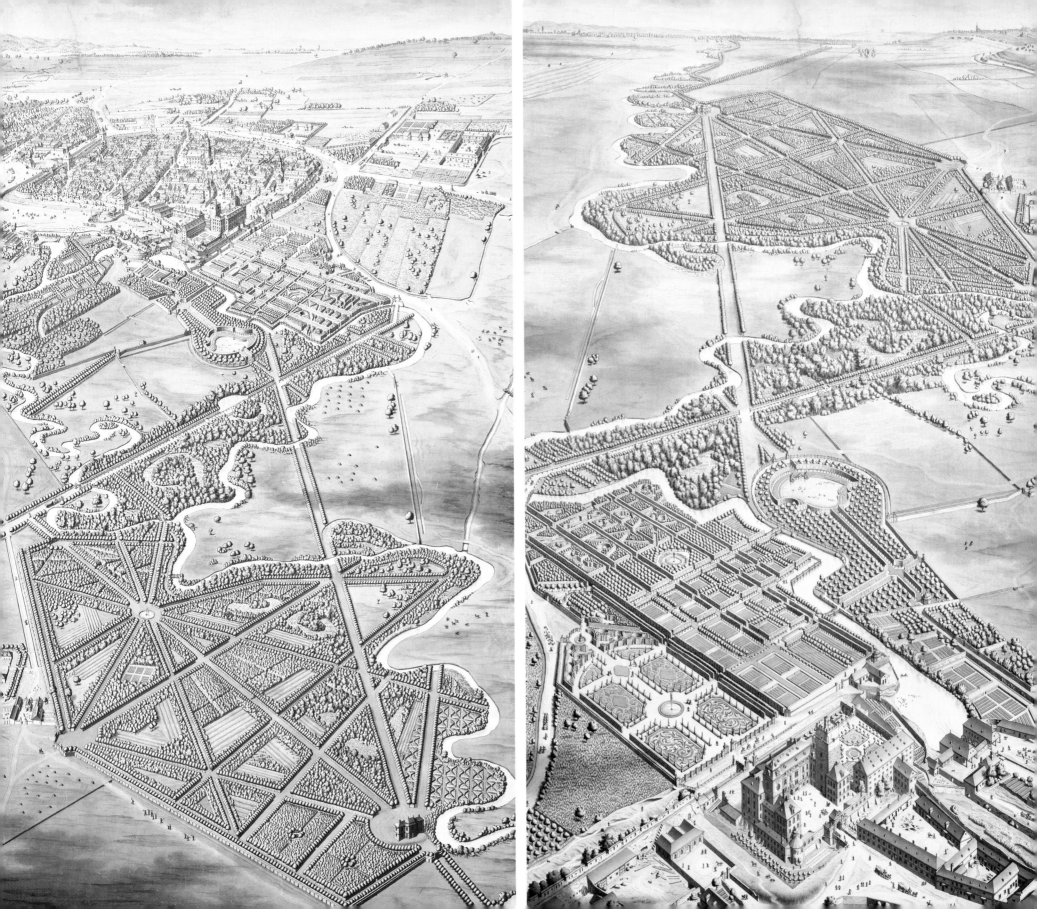

Opposite: The garden of Schloss Bruck
Bruck an der Leitha, Austria
Built around 1710 from plans by Johann Lukas von Hildebrandt for Count Alois Thomas Harrach.
Pen-and-ink drawings with gray wash colors, showing the completed grounds.

View of the Upper Belvedere
Vienna-Landstrasse, Austria
Built in 1700–1721 for Prince Eugen of Savoy, according to a design by Johann Lukas von Hildebrandt.
Garden laid out by "Fontainier" Dominique Girard.

Right: Apollo and Fire. First quarter of the eighteenth century

Below: View from the Lower to the Upper Belvedere

Gartenpalais Liechtenstein
Wien-Rossau, Austria
First master plan developed in 1688 by Johann Bernhard Fischer von Erlach for Prince Johann Adam Andreas I of Liechtenstein. Belvedere constructed in 1689 by Joahnn Fischer von Erlach. Garden palace built in 1692–1712 by Domenico Martinelli. Garden laid out by Jean Trehet. Garden sculptures from the mid-1690s by Giovanni Giuliani.

Left and below: Bird's-eye view of the garden toward the Belvedere, and bird's-eye view of the complete garden and the settlement of Liechtenthal. Pen-and-ink drawings with gray wash colors by Salomon Kleiner, 1732.

Right: View from the Belvedere through the garden to the summer palace. Oil painting by Bernardo Bellotto, 1758.

Sculpture garden and theater in the park of Schloss Salaberg
Salaberg-Stadt Haag, Austria
Laid out for Imperial Count Franz Ferdinand von Salberg.
Sculptures commissioned from Giovanni Stanetti in 1705.

Castle park in Schwetzingen
Schwetzingen, Germany
Laid out by Nicholas de Pigage (from 1762) and Friedrich Ludwig von Sckell
(English garden from 1774) for Prince Elector Carl Theodor of the Palatinate

Left: The serpentine stream of the birdbath in the northern Angloise

Above: The trelliswork ("Perspective") around the bird fountain at the bathhouse

Below: The natural theater in front of the Temple of Apollo

Opposite: Parterre bordered by arcades

Opposite and right: Perimeter fence for the large pond of Schloss Seehof Memmingen, Germany
Original Baroque park constructed in 1686, according to a design of Antonio Petrini. Built for Prince Bishop Lothar Franz von Schönborn as a summer residence for the Prince Bishops of Bamberg. Significant alterations in 1757 for Prince Bishop Adam Friedrich von Seinsheim. Furnished with sculptures in 1779 by the Bamberg court sculptor, Ferdinand Tietz.

Below and far right: Schloss Veltrusy. Fence and Baroque garden sculptures protected in winter by wicker baskets. Veltrusy, Czech Republic
Original castle erected in 1716 for Count Wenzel Chotek von Chotkow. Significant alterations in 1764.

*Nymphenbad (Nymphs' Bath) in the Zwinger
Dresden, Germany
Built by Matthäus Daniel Poppelmann (first project
1709, final realization 1711–1728) for August the
Strong. Completion of the Baroque ensemble through
the construction of a museum connected to the Zwinger
in 1854 by the architect Gottfried Semper. Sculptures by
Balthasar Permoser, Johann Christian Kirchner, Johann
Benjamin Thomaes, and Paul Egell.*

Schloss Weikersheim
Weikersheim, Germany
Garden laid out 1707–1725 according to a design by Daniel Matthieu.
Orangerie constructed by Johann Christian Lüttich, 1719–1723. Sculptures,
created in 1708, in part after engravings of Jacques Callot, by Johann Jakob
Sommer for Count Carl Ludwig von Hohenlohe.

Opposite: Buchlovice Castle
Buchlovice-Zlink'y Kraj, Czech Republic
Main wing of the castle built in 1702 by Domenico Martinelli for Johann
Dietrich von Peterswald. Parallel wing constructed behind and above the castle in
1710–1738. Baroque garden partially transformed into a landscaped garden in
the nineteenth century.

Palais Het Loo
Apeldoorn, Netherlands
Constructed in 1685–1692 by Jacob Roman and Daniel Marot for
Staatholder William III of Orange

Park of Peterhof Palace
Saint Petersburg, Russia
Planning by Tsar Peter the Great in 1716 in consultation with architects
Jean-Baptiste Alexandre Le Blond, Niccolo Michetti, Andreas Schlüter, and
Johann Friedrich Braunstein. Expansion of the Great Palace in 1747–1752 by
Bartolomeo Francesco Rastrelli under Czarina Elizabeth.

Left: The Golden Cascade with canal to the Gulf of Finland

Below top: The Hermitage Palace on the Gulf of Finland. Constructed in 1725
by Johann Friedrich Braunstein.

Below bottom: The Eve Fountain. Sculpture by Giovanni Bonazza (1718)
after the original of Antonio Rizzi (Doges Palace, Venice). Architecture by
Niccolo Michetti (1722).

Opposite: Triton Fountain in front of the Orangerie, erected 1726

Villa Pisani
Stra, Italy
Girolamo Frigimelica de' Roberti, commissioned in 1720 by Almorò Pisani. Villa completed by Francesco Maria Preti (1736–1756) for Alvise Pisani, Venetian ambassador to the French Court and elected doge in 1735.

Left: Belvedere on the garden wall

Below: View from the porch of the stables toward the villa

Right: View from the villa to the stables over the Great Canal built in 1911

Garden of Hampton Court Palace
East Molesley, England
Garden laid out in 1995, according to a design of 1702 as a re-creation of the original garden of King William III of England

Left: View over the Privy Garden toward the palace, designed by Sir Christopher Wren and erected in 1700

Below: View over the Pond Gardens

Right: View from the Great Fountain Garden toward the Great Canal with the Jubilee Fountain, created in the 1660s by King Charles II as a present for his bride, Catherine of Braganza. The Jubilee Fountain was restored in 2004 by Prince Charles.

THE WORLD AS MARVEL AND HARMONY

The Chinese Garden

The collision between the two great garden traditions, the European and the Far Eastern, occurred for the first time indirectly in Beijing. The French Jesuit Father Jean-Denis Attiret (1702–1768) worked there. He had studied painting in Rome and had moved to China in 1737 as a painter and a missionary. There, he worked for Emperor Qianlong (1711–1799) and submitted entirely to the ideas of his employer, who reigned over the country from 1737 to 1796. The first publication on the Chinese garden appeared in 1749, based on letters that Father Attiret had sent to Paris, and was printed in an English translation in 1752. In addition to depicting objects of Chinese fashion, the book *Le Jardin Anglo-Chinois*, which was published in several sequels from 1770 to 1787, also displays more than a hundred gardens of China's rulers. These reports were a sensation in Europe, yet one can imagine the impact these perceptions and experiences had on the Jesuit missionaries in China. They were accustomed to the axes and straight lines of Versailles, and its derivatives, which were shaped by unswerving avenues and waterways hundreds of feet in length. In China, the Europeans now experienced the exact opposite effect. They were able to visit the enormous Yuan Ming Yuan garden (Garden of Perfection and Light, or Garden of Sublime Clarity) of the emperor's summer palace, which the garden-obsessed Emperor Qianlong had commissioned and indefatigably continued to expand (a vast complex of lakes and palaces was sealed off to the outside world by means of giant walls). It encompassed approximately 140 buildings on an area of around 865 acres. A tiny part of it was occupied by the Xi Yang Lou palace, which Qianlong had built in the European style, according to the instructions of his European painters and artists.

Yuan Ming Yuan was probably the greatest pleasure garden ever built. As a European, one says this with special admiration. It was the most humane garden, the one that most closely corresponded to the nature of human beings. Today only marginal remnants of it exist, which here and there bespeak its incredible aspiration—especially the almost inconceivable dimensions it once possessed. The entire garden was repeatedly plundered and systematically destroyed in the course of the First Opium War in 1860 by an English division of the Anglo-French invasion army under James Bruce, eighth Earl of Elgin (1811–1863), in one of the most disgraceful actions of European imperialism.

Father Attiret's descriptions of the garden in his letters suggest wide stretches of natural terrain with, as he notes, clear bodies of water meandering through entwined valley landscapes separated from one another by narrow hills. Father Attiret describes the exciting rock formations that line the banks of these streams, and he is full of admiration for the fact that although he knows all this to be the work of human beings, this remains concealed and cannot be perceived. In each landscape section there were extraordinary buildings, all of them furnished with works of art and books. Many of these pavilions were only accessible by bridges. These were oftentimes also adorned with works of art and lookout pavilions that invited the visitors to pause at the right moment and take in the most beautiful panoramic scenes unfolding in front of them. "However, the most delightful sight is an island or a rock in the middle of the lake. . . . A small palace that contains at least one hundred different rooms is situated on this rock. . . . From there, one enjoys a view of all the palaces that are spread out around the shore of the lake at some distance; of all the hills that slope down to this shore; of all the streams that flow toward them . . . of all the bridges, regardless of whether they are located at the mouth of these small rivers or at the other end; of all the pavilions and triumphal arches that adorn the bridges; of all the woods that have been planted in order to separate and shield the palaces from each other."

If one has ever walked through these garden grounds, which are still enormous—although nowadays no more than a negative of what they used to be—one realizes the extent of the admiration and fascination that speaks from Father Attiret's description and how much even someone who was familiar with Versailles must have been impressed by the dimensions of this park alone. Added to this impression was the awe about the entirely different concept, about the apparent disorder, which was in stark contrast to the absolute principle of order of the Western garden. Was a type of orderliness—with axes and right angles, with absolute symmetrical counterparts—foreign to the Eastern world? No, the Eastern world knew these design principles as well and applied them in houses and palaces, possibly even more consistently than any occidental architecture. Many of the temple installations are aligned like giant astronomical instruments, where even the slightest deviations from the aspired principles of order simply do not occur.

Rules of the game of an entirely different nature have always been applicable to the garden in China. Father Attiret had already recognized this when we wrote to Paris that the Chinese knew very well how to apply the rules of "order and disposition" in areas where it was important to them—just not in the garden. The absence of this type of order in their gardens was intentional, because they were striving for "a natural and untamed view of the area; for a place of refuge and not a palace shaped according to the rules of art." In the European model, the rigid grid of geometry had been consistently applied to the scenery. In contrast, China's almighty Emperor Qianlong respected nature and man as equal partners in his enormous summer palace Yuan Ming Yuan; straight lines and right angles remained reserved for those buildings that articulated the relationship between one human being and another.

This differentiated approach can be explained with Far Eastern philosophical fundamentals. Order in a Chinese house corresponded to Confucianism with its clear striving for a regulated organization of human society. In the garden, however, the teachings of Taoists prevailed, who demanded harmonious unity between nature and human beings. It was the goal of the Chinese garden to achieve this harmony of nature (earth, sky, rocks, water, buildings, pathways, and plants) and to create the sublime oneness of humans with these elements. The basis for this aim was the Taoist principle of yin and yang, which expresses the balance and harmony of two sides of the same condition (calmness and movement, light and shadow, hard and soft, and man and woman constitute such pairings); in the garden, the rock with the falling waters is the embodiment of masculinity; the quiet, reflective surface of the pond, the embodiment of femininity.

So far we have only discussed the emperor's garden; however, we should take note of the larger picture. The Chinese garden had evolved already in very early times and was sustained since the Han Dynasty (206 B.C.–220 A.D.) by a prosperous class that was able to realize itself and its prosperity in the world of gardens.

This class also included scholars, painters, and poets who created gardens in their works that were ultimately implemented. The development of art and garden always progressed in a parallel manner in China; whereas similar thoughts did not meet any resonance in Europe until the genesis of the English garden in the eighteenth century. Here, as well, the models from poets or painters were transferred to three-dimensionality through the medium of garden architecture. It is amazing how similar the concepts were in the two cultures—and yet, two very different types of gardens emerged. No Chinese person would have been able to understand the endlessly flowing lawns of the English garden; conversely, no English person would have been able to understand the density of Chinese parks, the ruggedly rising rock landscapes in the smallest areas, the narrowness of the small courtyards, and the tiny surfaces of water. This multitude of small elements is one of the typical characteristics of the Chinese garden. Regardless of whether it is an imperial or a private park, this can still best be experienced in the small gardens of Suzhou, a city founded around 500 B.C., with canals and a great variety of gardens that have been preserved to the present day.

In the Wang Shi Yuan garden (Garden of the Master of the Nets), a private garden from around 1770, one can immerse oneself into such a small garden world, which concomitantly is part of the small world of a Chinese courtyard house. One enters the house through a small corridor and continues on through small courtyards with modest dimensions. They are decorated with artificial rock formations; planted with few plants, such as bamboo; and they never give rise to the thought of monumentality. The courtyards are cobbled with small stones that have been arranged to form simple ornaments, in some cases entire artificial flower carpets. It is a cosmos in which the individual elements have not been lined up in an axial manner, but rather composed together in an entirely labyrinthine manner—a world in which one can never really determine one's current standpoint; there is no logic regarding how much farther the hike will go, what surprises might still be ahead. A world in which the density increases from one room to the next; a world that trains one's eye on humble things; a world in which apparently inconsequential items become protagonists. In these rooms, one sharpens one's eye for the small changes in everyday life and the brevity of existence within the eternally recurring transformation of nature. The images that are conjured here carry the visitor to faraway, wildly rugged and picturesque landscapes that have been reconstructed. Residents went out of their way to haul the most beautiful rocks over large distances in order to have the miracles of nature present in their gardens. Libraries and studies, which are often completely secluded or, as in this house, situated on the second floor, are a reflection of this connectedness with nature. Therein, the scholarly owners were able to retreat and to devote themselves to the meditation of writing poetry or the art of ink painting. These were grounds that corresponded to the very high cultural standard of their inhabitants. In this "profane" example, as in the imperial pleasure parks, these small rooms overflowing with art objects, drawings, and watercolor paintings—which in many cases were more than a thousand years old—can testify to the unique continuity of this culture.

Without a doubt, the focal point of the gardens are the large bodies of water that announce themselves to the attentive visitors long before they really emerge from the labyrinthine interior spaces, which they had just paced through, into an open area. Here, in the Garden of the Master of the Nets, it is in the library that one has the privilege of being able to intuit the continuously changing play between water and light before actually stepping outside. Standing in front of the pond, the visitor is surprised by its size. Its irregular configuration, which gives the illusion that it cannot be beheld in its entirety, encourages this effect. One is under the impression that it continues behind this corner, behind that pavilion. There is no clearly defined path leading around the pond or courtyard; one can always enter adjoining rooms, to emerge in a completely different spot. The visitor quickly loses a prescribed sense of direction and is continually encountering new elements not seen before. It is possible to cross over the pond via a bridge; and here, as well, it is not the route that is the destination, but rather the views seen while traversing; the impressions received on the way. As is often the case in China, the bridge is not straight, but rather zigzags, causing a continual shift in direction and point of view, resulting in a more intense and longer-lasting pleasure from the crossing. A mere 43,000 square feet are sufficient in this small garden to create the experience of the entire world of the Chinese courtyard house in relation to the larger garden world—without inducing boredom for even a moment. After a walking tour, not a single visitor will know which route he or she actually took and where he or she was, which indicates how intentionally confusing and ultimately miraculous is the design of the entire park.

A visit to one of these small gardens is sufficient for us to recognize their essential elements: rocks and water. The rock is a symbol for the three islands of immortality—Penglai, Yingzhou, and Fangzhang—shrouded in mystery, which Qin Shi Huangdi (259–210 B.C.), the first emperor of China, already unsuccessfully attempted to find with an expedition of young men and women. Han Wudi (156–87 B.C.) untied the knot by commissioning bewitching replicas of the islands, which were intended to lure the immortals. He hoped they would then reveal their secret of immortality. Large, strangely shaped boulders were revered like local gods. During the eleventh and the twelfth centuries, the voracity for extraordinary rock formations escalated into true petromania. The rock collection of the Emperor Huizong (1082–1135), the extent of which broke every mold, even ruined the state finances. During the eighteenth and nineteenth centuries, this petromania experienced another blossoming. Rocks and water thus became the most important symbols for the dwellings of immortals in Chinese gardens. *Shan shui*, literally translated "mountains and water," eventually became the term for *scenery*.

Forbidden City
Beijing, People's Republic of China
First buildings constructed in 1406–1420 under the third Ming emperor, Yongle. The seat of the Ming Dynasty until 1644. Subsequent residence for a short time of the peasant leader Li Zicheng.
In October 1644, the six-year-old Shunzhi was proclaimed the first emperor of the Qing Dynasty. After the Xinhai Revolution in 1911, Pu Yi, the last emperor of the Ming Dynasty, abdicated.
Opposite: Northern view from the Pavilion of Eternal Spring (Wanchun Ting), erected in 1749 by Emperor Qianlong, to the Coal Hill (Mei Shan) and over the Forbidden City. The Coal Hill is a panoramic mountain created by heaping the materials excavated from digging up the moats surrounding the Forbidden City. Coal for the Forbidden City was piled at the bottom of the hill.
Below: View from the Forbidden City toward the Coal Hill and the Tower of the Splendid Panorama (Qiwang Lou)

Forbidden City
Beijing, People's Republic of China
The Inner Golden River in front of the Gate of Supreme Harmony in
the First Courtyard of the Forbidden City, with five marble bridges.
The bridges symbolize the five virtues of Confucianism: filial piety,
humanity, honesty, sincerity, and wisdom.

Forbidden City
Beijing, People's Republic of China
Imperial Palace Garden (Yu Hua Yuan) at the northern end of the Forbidden City
Left: Viewing pavilion. In the foreground, a "landscape" with picturesque rock formations
Below and right: Teahouse (Pavilion of Ten Thousand Springs). On all four sides of the teahouse stand trees where two trunks have grown into one.

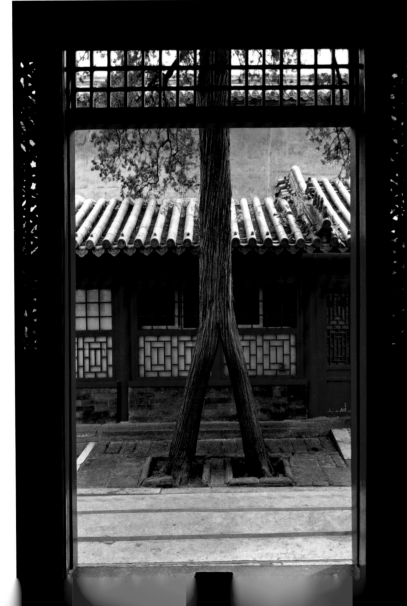

Forbidden City
Beijing, People's Republic of China

Opposite and right: Precious rock formations in the Imperial Palace Garden at the north end of the Forbidden City

Below: The Song of the Great Land of Wu. *Colored ink drawing by Lu Zhi, 1534. China's picturesque rock formations were models for rock formations found in gardens.*

Palaces on the eastern side of the Forbidden City
Beijing, People's Republic of China

Above: Wall panel (1417) with nine five-clawed dragons made of multicolored glazed clay bricks at the entrance to the Palace of Peaceful Longevity (Ning Shou Gong)

Left, below, and right: The Quianlong Gardens, laid out during the long regency of Quianlong (fourth emperor of the Qing Dynasty, regency 1735–1796/99). They render impressions of the inspection journeys of the emperor to south China (Jiangsu and Zhejiang). His most important counselor was the Jesuit Father Giuseppe Castiglione.

Garden of Harmonious Unity (Yihe Yuan) or New Summer Palace
Beijing, People's Republic of China
Given by Emperor Quianlong to his mother as a present on the occasion of her sixtieth birthday. Begun in 1751 and completed in 1764 on the site of the Garden of Pure Water (Jin-shui Yuan) that had existed since 1153. Destroyed during the Second Opium War and rebuilt from 1885 to 1895 by command of Cixi, widow of the emperor.

Below: View from the Temple of the Sea of Wisdom (Huihau Si) over the Pavilion of Buddhist Fragrance (Woxiang Ge) to Kunming Lake and South Lake Island (Nanhu Dao)

Right: View from the terrace of the Pavilion of Buddhist Fragrance (Woxiang Ge) over the roofs of the Hall that Dispels the Clouds (Paiyun Dian) to the gate of the Jade Palace, the Cloud Pillar (Paylou), and Kunming Lake

Garden of Harmonious Unity or New Summer Palace
Beijing, People's Republic of China
Left: Temple at the Pavilion of Buddhist Fragrance (Woxiang Ge)
Below: The garden with the Pavilion of Precious Clouds (Baoyun Ge),
cast from massive bronze
Right: View of the western wooded landscape of the New Summer Palace

Old Summer Palace (Yuan Ming Yuan)
Beijing, People's Republic of China
The Garden of Perfection and Light was once the
most elaborate and beautiful garden of China,
with approximately 100 landscape arrangements
and 140 garden buildings. Built for Emperor
Quianlong, partly under the influence of the Jesuits
Castiglione and Benoît and Bohemian missionaries,
in the European Baroque style. Completed in 1760
on the occasion of the twenty-fifth anniversary of the
regency of the emperor. Plundered and destroyed
in 1860 by a French-English punitive expedition
during the Second Opium War.

Left: Reconstructed labyrinth

Below and right: Remains of the monumental
fountains (Da Shui Fa)

135

Yuyuan Garden
Shanghai, People's Republic of China
Built as a private garden in 1559 by Pan Yunduan for his father
Pan En, a high official of the Ming Dynasty
Below: Almost endless variety of passageways
Right: View of the two-story Kuailou Pavilion

Garden of the Master of the Nets (Wangshi Yuan)
Suzhou, People's Republic of China
Constructed during the Song Dynasty in 1174–1189 for Shi Zhengzhi and restored in 1785 by
Song Zongyuan, a retired official of the Qing Dynasty. He gave the garden its name because he
wanted to show the life of a simple fisherman with his "pictures." A loggia for duck hunting and
a square pavilion stand next to the central pond.

Left: Garden of the Master of the Nets (Wangshi Yuan)
Suzhou, People's Republic of China
The courtyard in front of the Peony Study with the Cold Spring Pavilion

Below left: Garden of the Lion Grove (Shizi Lin)
Suzhou, People's Republic of China
Miniature gardens with strange rock formations and small bonsai trees bring
the landscapes of China into small courtyards.

Below: Quianlong gardens in the Forbidden City
Beijing, People's Republic of China
Door in the shape of a bottle and wall covered in colorful stone slabs

Silk with garden scenes. Originally a wall covering and later reworked into screens. Chinese silk embroidery, ca. 1780.

Left: Garden of the Master of the Nets (Wangshi Yuan)
Suzhou, People's Republic of China
View into the courtyard of the Barrier of Clouds Hall

Right: Villa della Regina
Turin, Italy
An overdoor in the western sleeping chamber with depiction of a
garden scene. Gouache on paper, ca. 1735.

Below: The Garden of the Humble Administrator/Foolish Politician
(Zhuozheng Yuan)
Suzhou, People's Republic of China
Stone mosaic in the Courtyard of the Chinese Flowering Apple Tree
(Malus spectabilis)

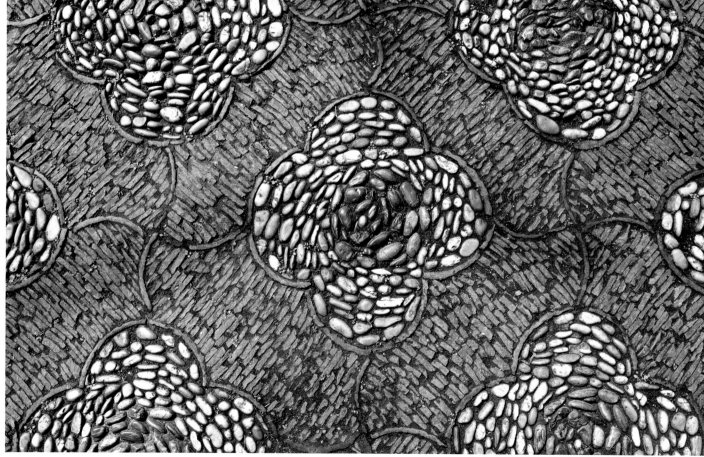

Left and below left: Views of and from the Remote Pavilion in the Garden of the Humble Administrator/Foolish Politician (Zhuozheng Yuan)
Suzhou, People's Republic of China
Laid out in 1509 by the Mandarin Wang Xianchen, it quickly became famous and was memorialized by the painter and poet Wen Zhengming in thirty-one album pages of verses and pictures.

Below right: View through one of the gates in the Garden of the Lion Grove (Shizi Lin)
Suzhou, People's Republic of China
Built in 1432 by his disciples for the Tianru monk Weize, who wrote fourteen poems with scenes from the Garden of the Lion Grove.
The famous poet and painter Ni Yunlin (Ming Dynasty) also took part in the creation of the garden and contributed to its fame.
The rocks of the garden depict lions in various forms and sizes.

Right: Stone bridge in the Garden of the Master of the Nets (Wangshi Yuan)
Suzhou, People's Republic of China

Below: The zigzag bridge to the Mingse Hall in the Garden of the Humble Administrator/Foolish Politician
(Zhuozheng Yuan)
Suzhou, People's Republic of China

FROM ABSTRACTION TO MEDITATION

The Japanese Garden

The genesis of the Japanese garden is unthinkable without prior developments in China. While the origin of the Chinese garden lies in the Han Dynasty (206 B.C.– 220 A.D.), the earliest Japanese gardens date from approximately 600 and, like Chinese gardens, are artifacts that imitate and reproduce nature.

It would be good to take time to examine the symbolism of the materials that are used in Japanese gardens. These are primarily stone, water, moss, and trees. The meanings conferred upon these elements are not consistent and are often ambiguous. Every garden is open to differing interpretations, no matter how meticulously it is planned. This openness to various possibilities is entirely in line with the worldview that underlies Japanese garden design. It is clear that the original temples have been renewed time and again, even up to the recent past, with a consciousness of tradition that is almost unimaginable to Western way of thinking. Thus, it is hardly surprising that content and interpretation have shifted over time.

The most important material in the Japanese garden is stone, capable of bearing a multiplicity of meanings. It can symbolize an island in the sea or an animal or gods who have descended from heaven. In the south garden of the Tofuku-ji Temple in Kyoto, four large rocks represent the Elysian Islands (Horai, Hojo, Eiju, Koryo) in the stormy sea (*hakkai*). On the western end there are five moss-covered mounds that stand for the Five Sacred Mountains (*gozan*). The original garden dates to the thirteenth century and was renovated in 1890; the ensemble was newly laid out in 1939 by the garden architect and scholar Mirei Shigemori (1896–1975).

The second element that appears and is employed again and again is raked gravel or pebbles. This represents the stormy sea, with its dynamic image of the waves. According to Taoism, it also symbolizes the home of the gods, who abide here. Sometimes the pebbles, trapped between the boulders, represent the mountain stream or the waterfall that plunges down into the valley or flows under a bridge. This is seen in the rock garden of the Zuiho-in Garden in Kyoto, for example.

The third element that is used is moss, the principle symbol for age and honor. Here it is the symbol for the Five Sacred Mountains, which stand for the ten [sic!] most important Zen monasteries of Japan. This system of symbols was created in China during the Song Dynasty (960–1279) and brought to Japan during the Kamakura period (1186–1333). Five of the temples were located in Kamakura and five in Kyoto. They became important administrative bodies during the time of the Shogunate and enjoyed state support. The cultural importance of moss in Japan is either completely incomprehensible for a Westerner or simply stunning—there is almost nothing more beautiful than a bank of moss in the flat light of the evening sun.

Finally, the sorts of plants that we imagine when we think of a garden— shrubs and trees—are not present here. Deciduous trees, whether in their monumental, normally pruned form or as small bonsai in the courtyard or house, are symbols of human life or of the human condition itself. For this reason they are lavishly and laboriously tended until they die. The phrase "Honor old age," one of the principles of Western culture, has remained inviolable in Japan, as is evident in how trees are treated. The blooming of trees in the spring, and, above all, blossoms (*sakura*)—especially the beauty and impermanence of plum and cherry blossoms—are celebrated anew every year. They are the occasion for hundreds of thousands of people in Japan to travel to the place where this reawakening of nature

can be experienced in its most intense and powerful form, in Kyoto. Beginning in March in southern Kyushu, the "cherry blossom front" wanders northward, all the way to Hokkaido in the northeast in May. The gardens only achieve a comparable attractiveness at one other time in the year, when the leaves of the maples (*momiji*) and the gingkoes change color. Brilliant greens, reds, and yellows of an intensity seldom experienced in our latitudes entice people out into nature once more.

Evergreen bamboo, both pliant and stable at the same time, is another popular element in the garden. Its cane—marked by varied segments, thicknesses, and appearances—strives upward in layers that seem never to end as the years add ring upon ring. Regarded in this way, the bamboo becomes a perfect symbol for the generations of human life. Finally, this symbolism is not limited to individual objects alone, but also relates to the arrangement of various contrary pairs. The juxtaposition of the pine tree and the plum tree, for example, suggests the dualism that exists between the moment and transience.

A short look at the career of the aforementioned Mirei Shigemori, the most celebrated Japanese gardener of the twentieth century, makes clear the complexity and complicated nature of the history of the Japanese garden. As a young man he received training in the classical tea ceremony, in the arrangement of flowers (*ikebana*), and finally in landscape and ink painting. In 1917 he began studying classical Japanese painting and planned to found a comprehensive school for classical Japanese culture. These plans ended, however, with the Great Earthquake of 1923. At this time he became involved with the Japanese garden. In 1938 he completed the publication of a major work, *The History of the Japanese Garden*, in twenty-six volumes. A revised edition of this book was published in 1971, shortly before his death. He also designed gardens, beginning in 1914, with the garden of his own home. In 1939 he redesigned the garden of the Tofuku-ji Temple, mentioned above, after which 240 other gardens would follow. He was able to call upon not only his comprehensive knowledge of Japanese culture but also his familiarity with contemporary artistic trends to accomplish all these projects. He entertained a close relationship with architects, such as Kenzo Tange (1913–2005), who had discovered the possibilities inherent in historic Japanese architecture for modern artistic expression. Shigemori's subtle and profoundly creative encounter with the Japanese garden would not have been possible without his proximity to modern architectural trends.

Following this excursion into the immediate past, a look back into history reveals that gardens did not appear in Japan as early as they did in China. By the end of the seventh century, however, they had become common property. The Korean gardener known as Shikomaro, who created a number of impressive gardens in Japan, had attained considerable celebrity by the year 612. During the Nara period (710–794) and the Heian period that followed it (794–1185), the influence of poets and painters on garden design became increasingly important; the parallels to developments in China are unmistakable.

From the tenth through the twelfth centuries, gardens were usually laid out to the south of the living spaces in the palaces of the aristocracy. The focal point of the garden was a pond with a mound in the background. The Joju Temple, at the foot of Mount Kiyomizu in Kyoto, possesses a garden from the fifteenth century that corresponds to this type of design. In a sense, these gardens were reflections of the cosmic order, but they also served as places of entertainment for the nobility. There was great enthusiasm for anything that came from China. Entire fishing villages were constructed beside ponds, and the ponds and canals were used for boating trips, during which poetry and music were performed by artists in Chinese dress. As in China, an intimate dialogue between poetry, music, and painting was seen in Japan. If the descriptions handed down can be believed, the ways that gardens were used were as varied and colorful as the ways they were laid out.

Soon after the Heian period, a general transition took place. The Kamakura period (1185–1333) began with the severing of relations with China and the foundation of a new capitol for the warrior government in Kamakura. Gardens were now much more frequently a part of monasteries rather than palaces or private residences. Financial investment in garden design was reduced even further in the following Muromachi period (1333–1573), due to the influence of the art of ink painting in the Song Dynasty (960–1279) of China. The gardens were now intended to be as monochromatic as ink-painting landscapes. The most important gardens of this period were in Kyoto: Tenryu-ji (the Temple of the Heavenly Dragon Garden, laid out ca. 1339), representing the transition from the Shinden style to the Zen style; Kinkaku-ji (the Garden of the Golden Pavilion, laid out 1397); and Ginkaku-ji (the Garden of the Silver Pavilion, laid out 1484).

A process of "petrification" began in the Japanese Middle Ages as a result of these financial constraints. Under the influence of Zen Buddhism and contemporary landscape painting, plants were increasingly banished from gardens and the ultimate result was a completely flat design. Gardens lay spread out before the rooms of the monks like picturesque works of art to be meditated upon. So began the triumphal procession of stone gardens (*kare-san-sui*) intended for meditation alone. These stone gardens are seen as likenesses of the world. One is meant to sit in meditative wonder before rivers and waterfalls formed from pebbles, the seas created by these rivers and falls, and before the islands and mountains of the gardens. Such panoramas, where an entire cosmos is frozen in time, have been handed down since the sixteenth century by the temple gardens Daisen-in and Ryoan-ji of Kyoto.

The type of Japanese garden reaches its culmination in these Zen gardens. This is not a garden like a Western landscaped garden, where a person can walk around for days. The Japanese garden, irrespective of when it was created, is a garden of precisely framed pictures where people enter and remain silent until they reach the next picture, assuming there is another. The Japanese garden brings nature and human creation into closer juxtaposition than does any other kind of garden. No other attains such a high level of abstraction and stylization in becoming a living work of art. Nothing is left to chance in the Japanese garden. The smallest branch and moss cushion are governed by the gardener's creative thinking and care. There is no garden in which greater respect is paid to nature than in the Japanese garden, despite the evidence of extreme human intervention in nature that it displays. For generations, hedges in European gardens have been clipped and formed using large scaffold structures and giant machines. The Japanese gardener deliberates about how and where to act before he makes the tiniest cut to

give the tree its final form, in order that his intervention and the growth of the tree will reach the desired goal in perfect harmony.

The tea garden came into being as an additional garden type with the development of the tea ceremony. The tea garden is not meant to be merely the object of meditation but something to be physically entered. The tea ceremony (*chado*) is a ritual that also began in China. Its structure was codified at the beginning of the twelfth century and is even today characterized by a fixed set of rules. The name given to the concept of the tea ceremony is already controversial, for it is neither a ceremony nor a ritual. It stands, rather, for a path of life and should probably be called the "tea path." The nature of the tea path is already evident in the arrangement of the buildings. It begins in the waiting room (*machiai*), usually an open pavilion. Here the guests gather and are greeted with a cup of mild tea by the host. Afterward they move to the teahouse (*chashitsu*) by way of a garden path (*roji*) that represents the first phase of enlightenment and the stripping away of everyday life. The teahouse itself is entered on one's knees (*nijiriguchi*), with an attitude of respect and humility, through an extremely low entryway closed off by a sliding door. This path is never laid out in a straight line, and there are particular illustrated models for it in instructional books. In *The Japanese House*, a book that is indispensable for understanding Japanese architectural history, the architect Tetsuro Yoshida (1894–1956) writes that "the most beautiful stones in Japanese gardens are the stepping-stones that come from tea gardens." He then goes on to precisely describe the rules for the placement of the stones, by which the natural and the artificial are to be interwoven.

The four underlying principles of the tea ceremony—harmony (*wa*), respect (*kei*), purity (*sei*), and tranquility (*jaku*)—also determine the construction of the teahouse and its garden. The longing for harmony ends in complete conformity with nature and an understanding for the impermanence of existence. These aspects of the tea ceremony are reflected in the construction of the teahouse and in the materials used: wood, bamboo, and clay. The house contains only two rooms, one for preparation and the other where the tea ceremony takes place. The main room has an area of 4.5 tatami (9 by 9 feet), corresponding to the dimensions of a rice mat (approximately 3 by 6 feet).

Further elements of the tea ceremony are the precious stone lanterns that are commonly encountered and stone water basins that are used for cleansing before the ceremony. Participants wash their hands and rinse their mouths, freeing themselves of the dust of everyday life. The majority of the vegetation is composed of evergreen plants, and conifers are very popular. Bamboo lends an impression of archaic primitive nature and evokes the eternal succession of generations. The moss that is found everywhere in Japan's humid climate grows rampantly on the ground. Larger complexes were also created by combining several such tea gardens. The garden of the imperial palace and, above all, that of the Katsura Imperial Villa in Kyoto are examples of this development that has continued to the present day. The Katsura Imperial Villa has even become an icon for modern European and American architecture.

Imperial Palace (Kyoto-Gosho)
Kyoto, Japan
First phase of construction simultaneous with declaration of Kyoto as capital in 794. From 1331 (accession of Emperor Kogon), as the Higashinotoin Tsuchimikado-dono Palace, it was the imperial residence until 1869. After the disastrous fires of 1788 and 1854, completely rebuilt within a year.
Above top: The Seiryo-den Garden and the Totei Garden with two different types of bamboo
Above bottom: Wall panels in the Sakura-no-ma (Cherry Blossom Hall)
Right: The Shishin-den Hall. In the foreground, the Dantei Gardens, with a mandarin orange tree and a plum tree.

The Oike-niwa Garden in the Imperial Palace (Kyoto-Gosho)
Kyoto, Japan
Laid out in the early Edo Period (1603–1868)

White and pink blossoming plum tree
Tenryu-ji Temple, Taho-den Shrine
Kyoto, Japan
Original park built in 1339 by Shogun Ashikaga
Takauji. Restored in the Meiji Period (1868–1912)
after a fire. Garden designed by Muso Soseki in the first
half of the thirteenth century.

Nijo Castle, Ninomaru Garden
Kyoto, Japan
The castle was built from 1603
for Shogun Ieyasu Tokugawa.
Expanded in 1626 under Shogun
Iemitsu. Wall paintings of the Kano
Schoool by Tanyu, Naonobu, and
Koui. Garden was designed by Kobori
Enshu in the late sixteenth and early
seventeenth centuries.

Opposite above: Wall panels with
cherry trees by Kano Naonobu, in
the Kuro-shoin Hall. First half of the
seventeenth century.

Below and below right: The Seiryu-en
Garden

Right: Lanterns in the Ninomaru
Garden

Left: Depiction of the Kiyomizudera Temple (founded 778) on a small Japanese lacquered cabinet. Second half of the seventeenth century. Urushi (black Japanese lacquer) with makie and nashiji decoration (gold and silver sprinkling).

Below: Lotus flowers in the pond of the Ryogen-in Temple in Kyoto, Japan

Right: Golden Pavilion (Kinkaku-ji) in the garden of the Rokuon-ji Temple
Kyoto, Japan
Original building constructed in 1397. Present-day temple rebuilt in 1955 after arson.

Villa Shisen-do (Hermitage)
Kyoto, Japan
Built in 1641 by and for the garden architect Jozan Ishikawa,
personal secretary of Ieyasu Tokugawa

Hojo-South Garden of the Ryogen-in Temple with its three classical Taoistic stone structures: Kame-shima (Turtle Island), Horai-san (Mount Horai), and Tsuru-shima (Crane Island)
Kyoto, Japan
Built by the priest Tokei. The garden was laid out in 1502 (Muromachi Period) by the painter and gardener Soami.

Rock garden in the Korin-in Temple, a subtemple of
the Daitoku-ji Temple
Kyoto, Japan
Built in 1521–1523 for Yoshifusa Hatekeyama

Rock Garden of the Ryoan-ji Temple
Kyoto, Japan
Originally the villa of the Tokudaiji family
(middle of the fifteenth century). Bequeathed
to Hosokawa Katsumoto. After his death
transformed into a Zen temple. Rock garden
with fifteen stones, created by the painter and
gardener Soami (1472–1525).

Rock Garden of the Zuiho-in Garden
Kyoto, Japan
Created in the Showa Period (1926–1989)

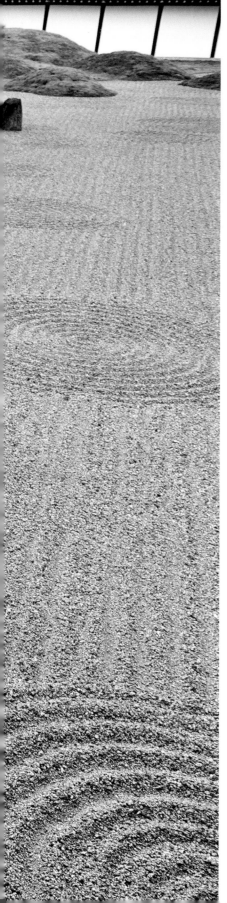

The Hasso Garden in front of the Hall of the Abbot (Hojo) at the Tofuku-ji Temple
Kyoto, Japan
The first temple was built by the priest Ennibenen in the middle of the twelfth century
and restored in 1890. Gardens rebuilt in 1939 by Mirei Shigemori. Only garden ensemble
where gardens completely surround hall.

Left, right, and right below: In the South Garden, four large rocks symbolize the Elysian
Islands (Horai, Hojo, Eiju, Koryo) in a stormy sea (hakkai) represented by pebbles.
On the western end are five moss-covered mounds—the five holy mountains (Gozan).

Below top: Chessboard pattern in gravel in front of the Kaisan-do Hall of the Tofuku-ji
Temple

Below bottom: In the East Garden (Hokuto-no-niwa), the stones of the foundation of the
original temple depict the zodiac sign of Ursa Major/Great Bear (Hokutoshichisei).

North and West Gardens surrounding the Hall of the Abbot at the Tofuku-ji Temple
Kyoto, Japan
The first temple was built by the priest Ennibenen in the middle of the twelfth century and restored in 1890. Gardens rebuilt in 1939 by Mirei Shigemori.

Left: North Garden with an irregular chessboard pattern, using the foundation stones of the former main gate

Right and below: West Garden with moss, pebbles, and quadratically trimmed azalea bushes

Garden with streams, bridges, and trimmed azalea bushes in front of the Kaisan-do Hall of the Tofuku-ji Temple
Kyoto, Japan

Garden of the Reiun-in Temple, a subtemple of the Tofuku-ji
Temple
Kyoto, Japan
Original garden laid out in 1390 by the priest Kiyo-honshu.
In the center stands a rock (Iai-seki) from the island of Kyushu
as a symbol of Mount Shumisen. The rock was brought here
in the mid-seventeenth century by Shosetsu. Restoration and
partial redesign of the garden in 1970–1971 by Mirei Shigemori,
according to historical depictions.

Garden of the Joju-in Temple at the foot of Mount Kiyomizu
Kyoto, Japan
Designed and begun in 1469–1487 by the painter and gardener Soami. Completed by the
gardener Kobori Enshu.
Left: A stone lantern in the background emphasizes the depth of the garden.
Below: A stone lantern (kagero) on the larger of the two islands, and a group of rocks
(Eboshi-iwa) that lean toward one another
Right: In the middle, a pond with two islands

Garden of the Heian-jingu Shrine
Kyoto, Japan
A memorial replica of the original garden of 794 with reduced dimensions, constructed on the occasion of the eleven hundredth anniversary of the original. The most representative example of the gardens of the Meiji Period (1868–1912).

Left: The Seiho-ike Pond (East Garden). In the background, the Taihei-kaku Bridge.

Below: View from the Taihei-kaku Bridge toward the guesthouse (Shobikan)

Right: The Taihei-kaku Bridge

Left and below: Stepping-stones for crossing the Soryu-ike Pond in the garden of the Heian-jingu Shrine Kyoto, Japan Constructed ca. 1900

Right: Bridge to the Castle of Matsumoto Matsumoto, Japan Japan's oldest extant castle. First building constructed in 1504–1508 by Shimadachi Sadanaga (Ogasawara family). After 1550 in possession of Ieyasu Tokugawa (founder of the Tokugawa Shogunate). Present-day building from the Bunroku Period, constructed in 1580 by the Isikawa family. Central tower erected in 1593/1594 by Ishikawa Yasunaga.

Left and below: Various kinds of moss
Kyoto, Japan

Right: Warabejizo statue of the Sanzen-in Temple,
covered by moss
Kyoto, Japan
First park laid out in the late eighth or early
ninth century

Left and below: Teahouse of the Okochi-sanso Villa Arashiyama-Kyoto, Japan
Villa of the Japanese silent film star Okochi Denjiri. Built in the second quarter of the twentieth century.

Right and below: A pine tree, more than five hundred years old, in the form of Mount Fuji. It stands near the Hosen-in Temple, a subtemple of the Shorin-in Temple. Ohara-Kyoto, Japan

Cottage (Rakushisha) with garden belonging to the poet Mukai
Kyorai, one of the ten disciples of the haiku poet Matsuo Basho
Kyoto, Japan
Built at the end of the seventeenth century (early Tokugawa Period)

Below: Fence made from rice straw and bamboo bound together at Korin-in Temple
Kyoto, Japan

Opposite: Fence made from rice straw and bamboo bound together at the
Imperial Palace (Kyoto-Gosho)
Kyoto, Japan

Left and below: Fern and anemone at the
Shisen-do Temple
Kyoto, Japan

Right: Stone fountain bowl at the
Enko-shi Temple
Kyoto, Japan

Zen garden with a fountain in the lesser garden of the
Hosen-in Temple, a subtemple of the Shorin-in Temple
Ohara-Kyoto, Japan

192

THE DESIGNED LANDSCAPE

The English Garden

The landscaped garden is still a reflection of paradise, even though the way it is conceptualized has changed radically. During the Middle Ages the idea of paradise was characterized by mathematical concepts. The sense of mathematical regularity translated seamlessly into the geometries of the Renaissance and then into the strictly ordered, absolutist worldview of the Baroque era. Subsequently, people began to imagine other possibilities for the landscaped garden. They became increasingly fascinated with the world beyond the confines of the gardens, with areas yet unshaped. They looked at the world of natural landscape and the ways in which mankind had transformed it in the course of human activity. There was no longer any interest in undeviating channels of water, but rather in carelessly meandering streams. Few cared about plants that were trimmed according to clear stereometric models (topiaries). Instead, people were more interested in the impressive growth of a tree in its natural state. This pleasure in the picturesque and the bizarre was one of the catalysts for new artistic developments in the Baroque and rococo periods wherein the irregularity of natural forms—of a shell or of a wild pearl, for example—were declared to be the ideal. A fascination with the exotic and the foreign was something that the Baroque had already discovered: Johann Bernhard Fischer von Erlach (1656–1723) published his famous *Entwurff Einer Historischen Architektur* (A Plan of Civil and Historical Architecture), the world's first inclusive study of architectural history, in 1721. Among the examples of Chinese constructions, he also included irregular rock formations that he called "Chinese pleasure mountains with caves and chambers." By including these, Fischer von Erlach appeared to be far ahead of his time yet was still in line with aspects of the Baroque. He was at least theoretically interested in a completely different world of formal conception, which he discussed in his history.

The buildings of Andrea Palladio were designed in accordance to an ingenious canon of proportion. In 1624 the English ambassador to Venice, Henry Wotton (1568–1639), stated that the gardens of Palladio's buildings needed to be the absolute opposite of this architecture. Sir William Temple (1628–1699), in an essay, "Upon the Gardens of Epicurus," written in 1685, pointed out the quality of the irregular in Chinese art as well as its disregard for European symmetry and uniformity. In the end, however, Temple was in favor of the European way because it would be impossible to make any truly glaring errors if the architecture was based upon geometry.

The painters Nicolas Poussin (1594–1665), Claude Lorrain (1600–1682), Gaspard Dughet (1615–1675), and Salvator Rosa (1615–1673) also immersed themselves in this new conception of the world and created paintings that became, even more than nature itself, ideals for the new designs. Landscape alone was discovered to be a paradise: suffused with light, covered with gentle meadows, traversed by gently flowing brooks and streams. In such pictures, and in the mythological history that they encompassed, human beings became incidental.

The ancient world was now seen with a new focus. Attention began to be paid to the tiny landscape pictures that were brought to light in ever greater numbers during the excavations of ancient Roman villas and palaces, rather than to the rigorous orders of columns. Illusionistic, almost impressionistic, views, light as a whisper, present a world that is an alternative to what had previously been thought most interesting in ancient culture. Nature and freedom became synonymous, and were soon associated concepts in politics and art, as well. The concept of freedom was postulated as a natural right; unspoiled nature became the symbol par excellence of freedom. The poet Alexander Pope (1688–1744) described trimmed plants as "ridiculous evergreen sculptures" and equated them with courtiers who had been "cropped" by etiquette. He declared the tree growing in nature to be a symbol of the free human being. Finally, Jean-Jacques Rousseau (1712–1778) considered clipping to be a metaphor for false education; he equated a good educator with a gardener attuned to nature.

In light of this it is easy to explain why the progressive minds of the age embraced the idea of the landscaped garden. The triumphal success throughout Europe of the landscaped garden—known even at this time as the English park— was also furthered by the excesses of the French Revolution that, while thirsting for freedom, managed to destroy most of the existing French gardens.

Artists like Hubert Robert (1733–1808) composed paintings that looked like gardens, and gardens that resembled landscapes. Natural, sculptural, and architectural elements, as well as architectural allusions, became aspects of the scenery. The architecture is no longer the stable element around which the overall composition revolves, as it was in the Baroque era, but simply a backdrop and conveyor of atmosphere. Style is no longer important. The world of antiquity, the Orient, even the European Middle Ages in its Gothic form—all of these can exist in well-balanced and immediate proximity to one another as purveyors of mood. And so, by the end of the eighteenth century, garden design had achieved undisputed primacy among the arts as a total work of art to which painting, sculpture, and architecture were subordinated. Garden design became an art form that oscillated between the dreamlike images of a distant Arcadia and the Utopia that the designer was attempting to realize. There was, however, often a dichotomy between the attempted realization of the Utopia and the concrete possibilities, as many of the great garden designers quickly discovered when their creative dreams dissipated.

There were certainly compelling political reasons for the development of Utopias, at least in the beginning. The coronation of George I, the first Hanoverian king of England, in 1714, did not lead to the desired reforms. There was public opposition to the mismanagement and corruption of the prime minister, Sir Robert Walpole (1676–1745), that led to the founding of the Country Party, an organization that united all those who resisted the deplorable state of affairs. City and countryside were seen as moral opposites, a dichotomy first made famous in one of the odes of Horace, *Beatus ille qui procul negotiis* (Happy the one far from affairs of business). The dissidents found intellectual and spiritual solidarity in the lodges of Freemasonry (the London Grand Lodge was founded in 1717), an organization also influential in disseminating the idea of the landscaped garden.

Alexander Pope was one person who was driven from the city into the countryside by political developments. He retired to Twickenham, near London, and purchased a house with a garden on the Thames in 1718. Ensconced in a villa with a grotto and a garden, he created the perfect ambience from which to propagate his vision of an immaculate and ideal England. Through his efforts he became a popular hero; in 1729, after returning from a trip to England, Voltaire reported that he had seen a portrait of Pope hanging in at least twenty villas.

Richard Boyle, third Earl of Burlington (1694–1753), was a good friend of Pope's and a member of a Masonic lodge. He owned the property Chiswick, halfway between Twickenham and London. There he built an "annex" to his villa in free imitation of the Villa Rocca Pisana in Lonigo, near Vicenza. This addition was intended as a rationalist statement of opposition to the Royal Court. Far removed from the Baroque craving for representation, it served as a meeting place for Boyle and his friends. The garden itself has many architectural allusions, almost as if intended as an open-air museum of ancient architecture. Boyle himself was the initial creator of this design. He was later joined by William Kent (1684–1748), recently returned from Rome, who through his designs became the driving force behind the creation of many gardens. At Chiswick he erected a miniature copy of the Roman Pantheon next to a tiny pond with an obelisk in its middle. Encircling the pond, planted in boxes, were lemon and orange trees that served as reminders of the south. Kent's creativity reached its first culmination in Stowe, where he worked for Richard Temple (1675–1749) from 1730 and onward and redesigned the rather stiff park that Charles Bridgeman (1690–1738) had begun there in 1716. He enlarged the grounds with the so-called Elysian Fields, thereby creating the first park that truly could be called an English landscape garden.

The second great figure of English garden design, Lancelot Brown (1716–1783), also began his career in Stowe. He was often called Capability Brown because it was said that he possessed the ability to recognize possibilities inherent in any location for the creation of a landscaped garden. While an assistant gardener and kitchen gardener, he led the English nobility through the park at Chiswick, then created his first plans under the tutelage of William Kent. In 1750 he designed the grounds of Warwick Castle, an accomplishment that gained him immediate fame. The grounds of Blenheim, the country estate of the Dukes of Marlborough, followed in 1764, and in 1767 he took up the post of master gardener at Hampton Court, just to mention a few of the cornerstones of his incomparable career.

In addition to sociopolitical considerations, concrete economic factors certainly played a decisive role in the establishment of the new style. A large French garden required enormous expenditures and an army of gardeners to maintain; consequently, many gardens became ruins within a short time after their creation. Landscaped gardens, on the other hand, were capable of easier integration into the cycle of estate life and economics. Ideally, garden design and agriculture could join together in balance and harmony to form an ornamental farm. Gardens had a realistic chance of survival only if this balance was actually maintained.

Thus, it was only a matter of time before the fashion of the landscaped garden was embraced throughout Europe. France followed England in an attempt to break with the rituals of the Baroque period. In the works of the painter Antoine Watteau, (1684–1721), whose theme was so often the courtly garden parties of the nobility, scarcely a picture presents a formal garden as the venue; with few exceptions, a setting in intimate contact with nature serves as the backdrop, revealing Watteau's paintings to be far ahead of their time. Make-believe country life becomes reality at the Hameau (1782–1789), Marie Antoinette's little village at the Petit Trianon on the palace grounds of Versailles. The tiny group of peasant cottages and fishermen's huts becomes the prototype for all comparable later ensembles. France also saw the

invention of the *jardin anglo-chinois* (Anglo-Chinese garden), inspired by descriptions of Chinese gardens published by the Jesuits Jean-Baptiste du Halde (*Déscription de la Chine* [Description of China],1735) and Jean-Denise Attiret (1749). Pavilions, kiosks, and pagodas became fashionable, as did artificially picturesque rock formations and delicate little bridges connecting islets with the shore. This fashion quickly incorporated a retrospective of antiquity; the pagoda of Chanteloup (1775–1778) owes the shape of its plinth level to the ancient monopteros. With the creation of the Parc Monceau that the poet Louis Carrogis Carmontelle (1717–1806) began in 1773 for Louis-Philippe-Joseph, Duke of Orleans (1747–1793), there arose an unrestrained evocation of motifs from ancient Egypt, classical antiquity, the Orient, the Netherlands, and even the Swiss Alps.

The garden of the Marquis de Girardin (1735–1808) in Ermenonville achieved decisive importance. Girardin was a patron of Jean-Jacques Rousseau, who spent the last weeks of his life in Ermenonville. Girardin opposed the appropriation of the English model, as had occurred in the *jardin anglo-chinois*, and created a garden full of the spacious vistas of Arcadian landscapes. In a treatise on gardens published in 1777, he provided additional new approaches by demanding the marriage of beauty and usefulness. This was a demand followed by the revolutionary classicists, whose monuments never remained empty forms but were always filled with concrete content. The designs that Claude Nicholas Ledoux (1736–1806) created around 1780 for the Marquis de Montesquiou's landscaped garden Maupertuis were legendary: the ball on the House of the Game Warden symbolized the vigilance exercised in all directions, the House of the Inspectors of the River Loue lay like a circlet around the waterway under surveillance.

The first English garden in Germany was begun in 1764, after the twenty-four-year-old Prince Leopold III Friedrich Franz von Anhalt-Dessau (1740–1814); his friend the architect Baron Friedrich Wilhelm von Erdmannsdorf (1736–1800); and the thirty-year-old court gardener Johann Friedrich Eyserbeck (1734–1818) returned from a long journey to England. There they had studied garden culture and agriculture, but also the latest industrial developments. Shortly afterward, the Garden Kingdom of Wörlitz—an ensemble of parks, woods, and meadows that radiated its beauty as far as Dessau and Oranienbaum—was created. It quickly became a place of pilgrimage for Central and Eastern Europeans who were interested in garden design. The development of the English garden extends far into the nineteenth century, as is visible in the gardens of Prince Hermann Ludwig Pückler-Muskau (1785–1871) in Branitz and Muskau.

The example of Wörlitz was soon followed in the parks of the Austrian imperial house in Laxenburg, and in the extensive country estates of the Austrian nobility, whether in their ancestral homeland or in Bohemia, Moravia, or Hungary. The Liechtensteins, the Schwarzenbergs, the Auerspergs, the Choteks, and the Esterházys—all disseminated the new forms of design and, more important, of estate economics.

The gardens of Russia deserve mention in passing. A felicitous synthesis between the new ideals in garden design and the endless expanses of the Russian countryside was achieved in the parks of Pavlovsk and Pushkin, near Saint Petersburg, and later in the nineteenth century in the garden of the Arkhangelskoye estate near Moscow.

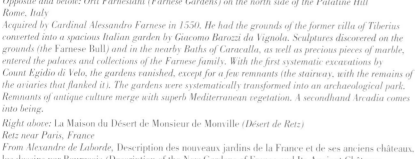

Opposite and below: Orti Farnesiani (Farnese Gardens) on the north side of the Palatine Hill
Rome, Italy
Acquired by Cardinal Alessandro Farnese in 1550. He had the grounds of the former villa of Tiberius
converted into a spacious Italian garden by Giacomo Barozzi da Vignola. Sculptures discovered on the
grounds (the Farnese Bull) and in the nearby Baths of Caracalla, as well as precious pieces of marble,
entered the palaces and collections of the Farnese family. With the first systematic excavations by
Count Egidio di Velo, the gardens vanished, except for a few remnants (the stairway, with the remains of
the aviaries that flanked it). The gardens were systematically transformed into an archaeological park.
Remnants of antique culture merge with superb Mediterranean vegetation. A secondhand Arcadia comes
into being.
Right above: La Maison du Désert de Monsieur de Monville (Désert de Retz)
Retz near Paris, France
From Alexandre de Laborde, Description des nouveaux jardins de la France et de ses anciens châteaux.
les dessins par Bourgeois (Description of the New Gardens of France and Its Ancient Châteaus.
Drawings by Bourgeois), *1808. Copperplate engraving.*

Right middle: Kilian Ponheimer, Aussicht des Predigtstuhls. Eines dem Russisch Kaiserl. Herrn
Botschaft in Wien Fürsten v. Galityin yugehörigen Landgutes (View of the Predigtstuhl. An Estate
Belonging to Prince Galitzin, the Russian Imperial Ambassador in Vienna),*1789. Copperplate engraving.*

Right below: Das Lzsikratesdenkmal in einer Phantasielandschaft am Meer (The Lysikrates Monument
in a Fantastic Landscape Beside the Sea). *From Georg Christoph Kilian,* Ruinen und Überbleibsel von
Athen (Ruins and Remnants of Athens), *1764. Copperplate engraving.*

Left: The tomb of Jean-Jacques Rousseau in the park of the castle of Ermenonville
Ermenonville, France
Colored copperplate engraving by Carl Ludwig Frommel, first quarter of the nineteenth century

Right: Three views of the park of Laeken Castle
Laeken-Brussels, Belgium
Castle and park constructed in 1781–1785, according to designs of Charles de Wailly by Louis Montoyer for the Austrian stadtholder in Brussels, Albert Kasimir von Sachsen-Teschen. Watercolors by Françoise Le Febvre, 1787.

The English Garden of the Petit Trianon with the village of Queen Marie-Antoinette at the Palace of Versailles
Versailles, France
The Petit Trianon was given to Marie-Antoinette in 1774 by her husband, King Louis XVI. Immediately afterward, transformation of part of the formal garden into a landscaped garden, and in 1783–1788, construction of a small rural village (hameau) by Richard Mique.

Left: The Marlborough Tower

Below and opposite above: The farm

Opposite below: View over the pond to the Marlborough Tower, the mill, and the Maison de la Reine (House of the Queen).

Chiswick House and grounds
Chiswick-London, England
Built in 1720–1730 by William Kent and Charles Bridgeman for Richard Boyle, third Earl of Burlington. Garden laid out by the royal gardeners William Kent and Charles Bridgeman, based on the model of landscape paintings of Arcadian Italy (e.g., by Nicolas Poussin and Claude Lorrain). Burlington had become acquainted with Kent and Bridgeman in Italy during his Grand Tour. In addition to the citation of antique models (architectural elements, trophies, sculptures) in the design of the grounds, there is a rejection of the axis as an organizing principle and the opening of the previously walled garden into the surrounding landscape. Chiswick was the birthplace of the English landscaped garden.

Left: The Ionic Temple and the Villa, completed in 1729

Opposite: The Ionic Temple (Pantheon) and Obelisk beside the round pond in the hollow of the Orange Tree Gardens. The area around the pond was originally occupied by small boxed orange trees.

Castle Howard
York, England
Built in 1669–1712 by Sir John Vanbrugh and Nicholas
Hawksmoor for the third Earl of Carlisle. Originally
contained formal gardens that were later transformed into
a landscaped garden with expansive bodies of water and
meadows that merge into open nature.

Left: Stourhead Gardens
Stourton, England
Stourhead House was built in 1721, following the model of Palladian villas, by Colin Campbell for the banker Henry Hoare. His son, Henry Hoare II, remodeled the garden after returning from a Grand Tour in the 1730s, with the help of the architect Henry Flitcroft. The younger Hoare was inspired by French and Italian landscape paintings (Nicolas Poussin, Claude Lorrain, Gaspar Dughet) of the sixteenth and seventeenth centuries and incorporated his impressions into the new design of the garden. Every view from the central lake should offer a new perspective.
View over the bridge to the Pantheon, built 1753/1754, that dominated the western bank

Below: Stowe Landscape Gardens
Stowe, England
Built for Richard Temple, first Viscount of Cobham, by Charles Bridgeman (from 1718), Sir John Vanbrugh (1721), William Kent (from 1730), and Capability Brown (from 1740)
The Great Obelisque

Stowe Landscape Gardens
Stowe, England
Below: *View from Stowe House over the Lake Pavilion (Sir John Vanbrugh, 1719) to the Corinthian Arch (Thomas Pitt, first Baron of Camelford, Lord Temple's cousin, 1765)*
Right: *The Monopteros (Temple of Ancient Virtue, by Sir John Vanbrugh, 1721)*

Stowe Landscape Gardens
Stowe, England
Left: Temple of the Queen (Ladies Building, by James Gibbs, after 1740)
Opposite above: The Gothic Temple (James Gibbs, 1741–1748) and the Palladian Bridge (James Gibbs, after 1740)

Wilton House
Wilton, England
First house in the Tudor style. Built in 1551 by William Herbert, first Earl of Pembroke. Modernization of the south wing in 1630 by Inigo Jones. The French parterre by Isaac de Caus (1632) is one of the earliest in England. Remodeled into an English landscaped garden in the eighteenth century.
Below: View of the house entrance with the Tudor tower
Opposite below: View of the Palladian Bridge above the River Nadder. Bridge erected in 1736/37 by Roger Morris for the ninth Earl of Pembroke.

Above: Frogmore House and Windsor Great Park
Windsor, England
House built in 1680. Purchased and remodeled in 1792 by King George III as a country
residence for Queen Charlotte. Garden redesigned in 1793 by Major William Price.

Left and opposite: Kenwood House
London-Hampstead, England
Existing house modernized in 1764–1779 by the architect Robert Adam for William Murray,
first Earl of Mansfield.

Pavlovsk. Garden and residence of Zarevich Paul (later Czar Paul I) and Maria Feodorovna (later Czarina Elizabeth I).
Leningrad Oblast, Russia
In 1777 Czarina Catherine I gave her son Paul land on the Slavianka River. In 1780 the English architect Charles Cameron was commissioned to build Pavlovsk. Construction began in 1782 and was completed in 1786.
Left and below top: Pavlovsk Palace
Below bottom: The Temple of Friendship on the Slavianka

Pushkin Palace and Garden
Zarskoye Selo-St. Petersburg, Russia
First selective expansion from 1717 under Czarina Catherine I.
Village renamed Zarskoye Selo by Czarina Elizabeth I (crowned in
1741). The Italian architect Bartolomeo Francesco Rastrelli was
entrusted with construction in 1749, and the heterogeneous group of
earlier buildings is unified. Under Czarina Catherine II there were both
French and English (from 1768) sections in Catherine Garden.
Alexander Park was constructed in 1818 by the Scottish architect Adam
Menelas (in Russia since 1779) as a spacious landscaped garden with a
Chinese village in the center.

Opposite: Detail of the Coral Bridge in Alexander Park

Right: The Palladian Bridge (Vasily Neyelov, 1770–1776) in
Catherine Garden

Below: The Chinese Bridge in Alexander Park

Views of the garden of the Esterházy Palace in Eisenstadt
Eisenstadt, Austria
Transformation of the Baroque garden and the palace into a neoclassical estate for Prince Nikolaus II von Esterházy by the French architect Charles de Moreau at the beginning of the nineteenth century
Left: Machine house on the Maschinenteich (Machine Pond)
Right above: View over the waterfall to the palace
Right middle: View of the garden facade of the palace, remodeled in the neoclassical style
Right below: View from the grotto to the large waterfall. Oil paintings by Albert Christoph Dies, 1812.

Garden of the imperial castle Schloss Laxenburg
Laxenburg near Vienna, Austria
Transformation of the original Baroque garden from 1780

Left: Emperor Franz and His Family at Laxenburg. *From* Hauptmomente aus dem Leben Sr. Majestät Franz I, Kaiser von Österreich apostol. Königs *(Great Moments from the Life of His Majesty Franz I, Emperor of Austria). Drawn by Johann Nepomuk Höchle, lithography by Franz Wolf, 1807.*

Below top: The Canal in the Park of Laxenburg Castle. From Wiens Umgebungen *(Vienna's Surroundings). Colored outline etching, 1827.*

Below bottom: The waterfall on the canal in the park of Laxenburg Castle

Garden of the imperial castle Schloss Laxenburg
Laxenburg near Vienna, Austria

Left: The New (Chinese) Pavilion in the park of
Schloss Laxenburg. From Wiens Umgebungen
(Vienna's Surroundings). Colored outline
etching, 1827.

Below and right: Present-day views after the
wartime destruction suffered in 1945.

The landscaped park in the Hinterbrühl
Mödling-Hinterbrühl near Vienna, Austria
Transformed into a landscaped park in 1808 by
Bernhard Petri and Philipp Prohaska for Prince Alois I
and Prince Johann I von Liechtenstein

*Left: The Colosseum (Amphitheater by Joseph
Hardtmuth, from 1810) at Mödling. Watercolor by
Jacob Alt, 1813.*

*Right above: The Colosseum at Mödling. From Wiens
Umgebungen (Vienna's Surroundings). Colored outline
etching, 1827.*

*Right bottom: View of the Amphitheater and
Liechtenstein Castle, the predecessor of the present-day
New Castle of 1820. Preliminary drawing by Laurenz
Janscha, engraved by Johann Ziegler. Colored outline
etching, last quarter of the eighteenth century.*

*Below: Die breite Föhre nächst der Brühl bei Mödling
(The Broad Pine by the Brühl near Mödling). Oil
painting by Ludwig Schnorr von Carolsfeld, 1838.*

The landscaped garden between Valtice and Lednice
Valtice-Lednice-Breclav-Pohansko, Czech Republic
Transformed into a landscaped park in 1792 by Prince Alois I and
Prince Johann I von Liechtenstein

Left: The Apollo Temple (Josef Kornhäusel, 1818–1820) in Valtice

Below: The Hunting Lodge of Pohansko (Joseph Hardtmuth, 1812)

Right: The Temple of Diana (Rendezvous. Joseph Hardtmuth, 1810.
Completed by Josef Kornhäusel, 1812) in Valtice.

The landscaped garden between Valtice and Lednice
Valtice-Lednice-Breclav-Pohansko, Czech Republic

Left above: The Temple of the Three Graces (Franz Josef Engel, 1825) in Hlohovec

Left: The Statue of the Three Graces (Johann Martin Fischer, last quarter of the eighteenth century) in front of the temple

Above: Colonnade on the Reisten (Jospeh Harthmuth in 1810, completed by Josef Kornhäusel, 1812) in Valtice

Right: Border House (Franz Josef Engel, 1816–1827) on the Bischofswarth Pond in Hlohovec. View from the southeast to the Border House. View from the terrace over the pond. Watercolors by Josef Höger, 1839.

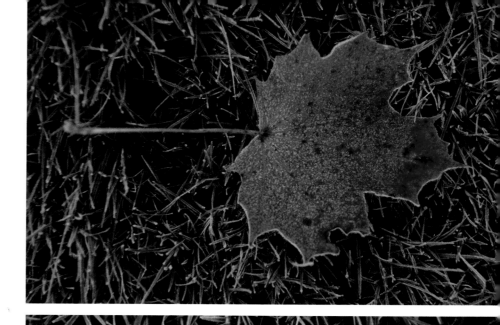

The spa landscape of Marienbad
Mariánske Lázne, Czech Republic
The first park laid out in 1807 by Johann
Joseph Nehr, the physician of the Tepl
Cloister. Extensive development from 1813
under leadership of Abbot Karl Kaspar
Reitenberger.

Left: The Ferdinand Spring. Built in 1826/27
with the support of Count Carl Chotek
over what was probably the first hot spring
discovered in Marienbad.

Right: Leaves covered by the first frost in the
spa park

Park of Kynžvart Castle
Kynžvart, Czech Republic
Built in 1821–1836 by Pietro Nobile for Prince Klemens Wenzel Lothar von Metternich-Winneburg zu Beilstein

Opposite and below left: In the castle park

Above: Castle from the courtyard side

Below right: Diana with the Hind. Copy of the Diana *from Versailles in cast iron. Created in the foundry of Count Karl Josef Salm-Reifferscheid in Blansko, north of Brno.*

235

Above: Prince Pückler Park
Bad Muskau, Germany
Splendid redesign of the garden on the Neisse River between 1815 and
1845 by Prince Hermann von Pückler-Muskau. The first renovation of the
castle, planned by Karl Friedrich von Schinkel, was never carried out. The
present appearance of the castle was determined by its renovation in the
Renaissance Revival style. This took place under Prince Friedrich of the
Netherlands (owner since 1846, owing to the financial difficulties
of Pückler-Muskau), with plans by Maximillian Franz Strasser and
Hermann Wentzel (1863–1866).

Left and opposite: The pyramids in Branitzer Park
Cottbus, Germany
Garden laid out in 1845 by Prince Hermann von Pückler-Muskau.
The artificial island with the pyramid stands in a lake fed by the Spree
River. The pyramid was created in 1856/57 as a burial site for the prince
and his wife, Lucie von Hardenberg, who had died in 1854.

Landscaped park in Machern
Machern, Germany
Laid out as one of the earliest English parks in Germany from 1782 by Johann Gottfried and Johann Christian Nehring for Imperial Count Carl Heinrich August von Lindenau

Left: Castle tower of the artificial ruins (1795/96)

Below: The Agnes Temple (after 1806) on the north shore of the Schwemmteich (flood pond).

Right: Pyramid as the tomb of the Lindenau family

The Wörlitz Garden Realm
Wörlitz, Germany
The eighteen-year-old Leopold III Friedrich Franz von Anhalt-Dessau assumed regency in 1758. In 1763 he took an educational journey to England with Friedrich Wilhelm von Erdmannsdorf. In 1765/66, he was on a Grand Tour of Italy, France, and Great Britain. From 1765–1813, he transformed the castle grounds into the first landscaped garden of continental Europe. Schloss Wörlitz constructed in 1769–1773 on the model of English country estates by Friedrich Wilhelm von Erdmannsdorf. First neoclassical castle in Germany.

Left and below: View from the stone (the Volcano) toward the village—with the tower of the parish church—and the castle

Right: The original furnishings (including furniture by Abraham and David Roentgen) and decorations from the time of construction have been completely preserved.

Wörlitz Garden Realm
Wörlitz, Germany
Built in 1765–1813 by Friedrich Wilhelm von Erdmannsdorf
Below: The Gothic House. Constructed from 1773 as one of the first neo-Gothic buildings on the European continent, after a visit to the English country estate Strawberry Hill (1764). Originally intended as a gardener's residence, from 1765–1813 it served as a private sanctuary (expanded several times) for the prince and Luise Schoch, the gardener's daughter, who had wed him in a morganatic marriage, and their three children. The windows have stained-glass paintings primarily produced in Switzerland between the fifteenth and seventeenth centuries.

The Volcano (stone) and the Villa Hamilton in Wörlitz, Germany
Built according to a design by Friedrich Wilhelm von Erdmannsdorf (1788–1794) as a memento of a journey to Naples and a monument to the prince's friendship with Sir William Hamilton, the British diplomat, collector of antiquities, and geologist
Below: View from the grotto under the Volcano toward the village
Opposite left: Villa Hamilton. In the background the Stone of Wörlitz (above). The Stone of Wörlitz (below). Watercolors by Karl Kuntz, 1797.
Opposite, right above: The top of the Volcano covered with colored glass
Opposite, right middle: Ceiling in a room with a fireplace in the Villa Hamilton
Opposite, right below: Grotto under the Volcano

The Wörlitz Garden Realm
Wörlitz, Germany
Built in 1765–1813 by Friedrich Wilhelm von Erdmannsdorf

Left and below: The Chinese (White) Bridge over the Wolfskanal where it empties into the Kleine Walloch, during the restoration of the bridge in 2007/08.

Opposite: The garden of the Luisium with the small castle and the White Bridge. Constructed in 1774–1778 by Friedrich Wilhelm von Erdmannsdorf for Prince Franz von Anhalt-Dessau for his consort, Louise. Named after her in 1780.

Left and below: The High Bridge in the park of Charlottenburg Palace
Berlin-Charlottenburg, Germany
Baroque garden laid out in 1697, probably by Siméon Godeau, a pupil of André Le Nôtre.
The garden was partially transformed into an English landscaped garden at the end of the
eighteenth century by Johann August Eyserbeck, a gardener from Wörlitz. The bridge over the
Carp Pond was manufactured in 1800 at the Royal Prussian Iron Foundry in the Silesian
town of Malapane (Ozimek) and erected in 1802. In 1832, the railings were modified to prevent
children from falling into the water.

Right: Arched bridges in the English-Chinese garden of Schloss Oranienbaum
Oranienbaum, Germany
Palace erected in 1683 as a summer residence for Henriette Catharina of Anhalt-Dessau.
Under Prince Leopold III Friedrich Franz von Anhalt-Dessau, the Baroque island garden was
transformed into an English-Chinese landscaped garden during the last quarter of the eighteenth
century. The new garden included a pagoda, a teahouse, and several arched bridges.

Glienecke Palace and Garden
Berlin-Steglitz-Zehlendorf, Germany
The new garden of Glienecke Palace was created
in 1823 by Karl Friedrich Schinkel and Ludwig
Persius, in close collaboration with the garden
architect Peter Joseph Lenné for Prince Carl, the
younger brother of Crown Prince Friedrich Wilhelm,
after Carl's return from his first journey to Italy
in 1822. The garden was laid out over the earlier
gardens of the counts of Lindenau (from 1796) and
Prince Karl August von Hardenberg (from 1814).

*Left: The Great Curiosity (Karl Friedrich Schinkel,
1835)*

*Below: View from the bank of the Havel River to the
Casino (Karl Friedrich Schinkel, 1824/25)*

*Opposite above: The Stipadium, an elevated seat with
a prospect of Potsdam (Ludwig Persius, 1840). In
front of the Stipadium, the monumental granite bowl
created by Christian Gottlieb Kantian.*

*Opposite below: View over the Casino to the Havel
River (Karl Friedrich Schinkel, 1824/25)*

Charlottenhof Manor on the grounds of Sanssouci Palace
Potsdam, Germany
Built upon an earlier structure in 1826–1829 by Karl Friedrich Schinkel and Ludwig Persius as a summer residence for
Crown Prince Friedrich Wilhelm of Prussia and his consort, Elisabeth Ludovika of Bavaria

Buildings in the park of Sanssouci Palace
Potsdam, Germany
Built between 1829 and 1840 by Karl Friedrich Schinkel
and construction supervisor Ludwig Persius. Ensemble
as a recollection of Schinkel's second journey to Italy in
1828. Gardener's house, 1829/30. Assistant gardener's
house in the style of Italian country houses. Roman Bath,
1834–1840. Tea Pavilion all'Antica, 1830.

English Garden of the Villa Borghese
Rome, Italy
Original Baroque garden of the Villa Borghese laid out in 1605 for Cardinal Scipione Borghese on the site of the ancient Horti Luculliani (Gardens of Lucullus). First steps to transform the garden into an English park in 1766 under Prince Marcantonio IV Borghese. Acquisition of further properties (Villa Giustiniani, Villa Pamphili, Villa Manfroni) by his son Camillo, husband of Paolina Buonaparte-Borghese, and his brother Francesco. The Giardino del Lago (Lake Garden) with the Temple of Aesculapius was laid out from 1785 to 1787 by the architects Antonio and Mario Asprucci. Continuation of this work and construction of many garden buildings at the beginning of the nineteenth century by Luigi Canina, an architect and archaeologist.

Villa Melzi d'Eril
Bellagio on Lake Como, Italy
Villa constructed in 1808–1815 by Giocondo Albertolli for Francesco Melzi d'Eril. Collaboration in the decoration by the painters Andrea Appiani and Giuseppe Bossi, as well as the sculptors Antonio Canova, Pompeo Marchesi, Luigi Manfredini, and Giovanni Battista Comolli (who created the gigantic bust of Emperor Franz in the park of Laxenburg Palace). Garden laid out, according to designs by Luigi Villoresi and Luigi Canonica.

Left: Bust of Pallas Athena

Below: View over the garden terrace to Lake Como

Right: Dante led by Beatrice to the heavenly regions (detail). Monumental group by Giovanni Battista Comolli.

CAPRICES OF IMAGINATION

Follies and Pavilions

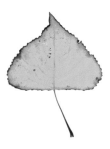

Follies—the buildings were named "foolish," as they did not make much sense in terms of their purpose if one assesses them from a functional standpoint. Yet huge amounts of money were invested in these items of "foolishness," and many of our gardens would have been headless, limbless torsos without them, both in the past as well as today. Particularly in the landscape garden of the second half of the eighteenth and the first half of the nineteenth century, follies virtually defined the essence of the garden. They set the atmosphere of a place and shaped its statement. However, their genesis as an important building type, which in most cases is not tied to a function, already began much earlier. Magnificent pavilions have always accompanied the history of gardens. Follies were especially open to change and innovation and were thus floodgates for the introduction of influences from China, Japan, India, Persia, Turkey, and many other cultures into the general repertoire of garden art.

Once more, the examination of the culture of the ancient world and its sites proved pivotal. The adoption occurred through the buildings or their ruins on the one hand, and on the other, through the works of ancient classical authors, in particular Vitruvius (Marcus Vitruvius Pollio, ca. 90–ca. 10 B.C.) and his *De architectura libri decem* (Ten Books on Architecture, 33–22 B.C.), which had only one flaw. There were no images whatsoever in the treatise. However, in the hands of creative minds, this perceived deficiency was quickly transformed into a positive effect: the lack of illustrations stimulated the imagination all the more and led to multiple attempts at interpretation.

If we look at the Roman murals in Pompeii, Herculaneum, and those discovered at other sites in their vicinity, we quickly see that there was also an abundance of garden architecture in the sense of pavilions, pleasure buildings, or pergolas in Hellenistic and Roman parks. Although such depictions most likely do not represent real situations, they nonetheless reflect a garden world that was full of gems. The designers of the Renaissance, with their reinterpretation of the culture of antiquity, included small pavilions and pleasure buildings in their garden repertoire and developed them further. Pirro Ligorio's (ca. 1510–1583) Casino for Pope Pius IV in the Gardens of the Vatican (around 1560) probably dates from the beginning of this period of adoption.

The first *peripteros*—Donato Bramante's (1444–1514) Tempietto in San Pietro in Montorio (ca. 1500)—soon found its way into the gardens and parks of the seventeenth and eighteenth centuries. The pavilion *all'antica* is thus a motif that emerged early and repeatedly in gardens; it was a "must," particularly in English parks, and was still counted among the most popular garden features well into the nineteenth and twentieth centuries. Grottos are another ornamental type; they have been inspiring the imagination since the Renaissance as hybrids between nature and art. They have often served as a backdrop for sculptures presented in a mysterious manner exclusively illuminated from the front.

The architecture of ruins constitutes a fascinating chapter. Already the first overall display of ancient Roman ruins, depicted in 1536 in the painting *Tempus edax rerum* (Time That Devours All Things) by Hermanus Posthumus (ca. 1512/14–before 1588), addressed the topic. In many instances, the remains of Rome are not represented realistically, or as they might actually have been experienced, but rather in compositions and arrangements that were in part quite fanciful. If they were installed as new in the garden, they were nonetheless portrayed as fragments and ruins in the painting. From then on, the fascination with ruins continued through all eras; gardens are full of artificial ruins: Greco-Roman, Gothic, or timeless ones.

Another type of "foolishness," which was also directly connected to the culture of antiquity, can be found in the gardens of the Medici around Florence; for example, Giambologna's (1529–1608) *Appennino* in the manor garden of Francesco I de Medici (1541–1587) in Pratolino from the middle of the sixteenth century. It features a statue that is so enormous that one can walk into it and look out through its eyes.

Even in Vicino Orsini's (1523–1585) Giardino delle Mostre in the Sacro Bosco of Bomarzo in Viterbo, there is an accumulation of such follies—sculptures of downright superhuman dimensions, which quickly turn into architecture; for example, a mouth through which one can easily walk. And finally, the Casa Obliqua is quite unique: a house that is askew in the true sense of the word and thus represents the idea of this garden. Its commissioner, Francesco Vicino Orsini—his secretary was Pirro Ligorio—wanted to escape from the order of rationality, the *ratio*, and to establish it beyond the logical mind in the borderland between life and death. It is a garden in which many things are askew, in which one can gain entirely new experiences—not only while fumbling through and quickly losing one's balance in the crooked house with the sloping floors.

In the French garden, the "askew" lives on in Versailles, where the battle of the giant, son of Gaia (Earth), in the frenzy of the water and thunderbolts twitching in his hands, is depicted in the Bosquet d'Encelade. In Germany, the *Herkules* of the Palace Schloss Wilhelmshöhe stands in the same tradition; he is also a folly—modeled after the ancient statue of *Herkules Farnese*—and was created in 1701 by the Italian sculptor Giovanni Francesco Guerniero (1665–1745) for Charles I, Landgrave of Hesse-Kassel (1654–1730).

In England, an attempt was made to accentuate individual points in English parks by means of follies in various forms and dimensions. This trend was started at Castle Howard, close to York, which was erected by John Vanbrugh (1664–1726)—also a playwright—and Nicholas Hawksmoor (1661–1736) for the third Earl of Carlisle. Here, a rotunda, a triumphal arch, and a gigantic mausoleum compete for the visitor's attention. The garden installations of Stowe became a classic where the painter, architect, and garden designer William Kent (1685–1748) grouped a plethora of such structures across the Elysian Fields that he had gently composed around a body of water in the valley. Each form of architectural expression can be found in these parks: from structures modeled on medieval examples to pavilions with origins in an exotic and remote Asia. In England, the range of types is codified: favorites are the round temple, with or without surrounding colonnades; the pantheon; the obelisk; and the Palladian bridge, which a short time later began to appear in varying garden designs from the extreme west of Europe on the British Isles, all the way to the ambitious parks of the Russian tsars.

In between—in geographic as well as chronological terms—lies France and the French Revolution of 1789, which with its revolutionary architecture and its *architecture parlante*, brought about a tremendous burst of development, despite abruptly suspending formal continuity. Only a few of the designs created during this time were realized—typical are, for example, the Ruin of a Doric Column or the "tent" in the Désert de Retz— however, their significance as inspiration for future developments cannot be overstated. In the royal parks of Haga and Drottningholm in Schweden, guard posts and supply points were housed in such tents designed by Louis Jean Desprez in 1787; wooden structures with a painted sheet-metal enclosure.

In Vienna, Joseph Hardtmuth (1758–1816) reacted to the developments of France's revolutionary architecture with his small, well-proportioned Voluptuar-bauten (voluptuary buildings), erected for the Liechtenstein family around the turn of the nineteenth century. In the woods surrounding the palaces Feldsberg and Eisgrub, he and his successors created many small architectural structures that continue to amaze even today: the colonnade on the Reistenberg Mountain; the Rendezvous (Diana Temple), close to Feldsberg; the Apollo Temple on the eastern side of Nimmersatt Lake, close to Eisgrub; or the Temple of the Three Graces by Hlohovec. A colonnade conceptualized as a ruin (no longer extant) stood north of Brünn in Adamsthal.

The most extreme level of folly can be seen in buildings influenced by Islamic or Far Eastern models, such as the Mosque in Eisgrub or in the estates of Hinter-brühl, south of Vienna—which were also owned by the Liechtensteins—or the Trojan Tower, which collapsed shortly before its completion and then was intended to be replaced by the architect Hardtmuth with a pyramid.

The mosque that Nicolas de Pigage (1723–1796) erected in the years 1779 to 1793 for Charles Theodore, Prince-Elector, Count Palatine (1724–1799) was the model for lavish excursions into the sphere of Islam. It was the most monumental and expensive of the follies in the garden of Schwetzingen and comprised the Jardin Turc, surrounded by an arcade passageway, and the mosque. The covered walk had more of the character of a cloister, and it has retained its contemplative atmosphere until today; the inevitable fountain, as well as the prayer niche and pulpit, are missing in the mosque, a clear link to occidental Christian architecture—St. Charles's Church, Vienna, in particular.

These buildings were preceded by the monumental seven-story Pagoda of Chanteloup, which Duke Étienne-François de Choiseul (1719–1785) had built as a *temple de fidélité* from 1773 to 1778 in the center of his park. It is one of the most delightful creations of the *jardin anglo-chinoise*, from which countless such structures derive—from the wooden pagoda based on the design of Sir William Chambers (1723–1796), which was completed in Kew Gardens in 1792, to the Chinese temples that abounded throughout France and Central Europe. Those buildings now house the Museums of the Far East in Laeken close to Brussels. The Japanese Tower was originally created for the World Exhibition in Paris in 1900 and impressed King Leopold II of Belgium so much that he commissioned a copy for the garden of the royal palace. He also placed a Chinese Pavilion next to it. For both, the decorations were made by local artists—in Japan for the tower, in Shanghai for the pavilion—which significantly contributed to their convincing, high-quality workmanship.

If we are to follow this theme up to the present, the Chinese Garden at Lake Zurich—a gift from the city of Kunming, inaugurated in 1994—could also be men-

tioned. Apparently, the unstoppable propagation of this fashion had already been foreseen by the author Sir Horace Walpole (1717–1797), who looked out onto the Kew Gardens pagoda from his estate in Twickenham on a daily basis and complained to a friend, "In a fortnight you will see it in Yorkshire."

Another major work expressing the longing for the East is the Royal Pavilion in Brighton, which was erected by the strict classicist John Nash (1752–1835) from 1815 to 1822 for the Prince of Wales, the future King George IV (1762–1830). The outside was characterized by domes reminiscent of Indian models, the inside was an Eldorado of Chinese ornaments. The summer pavilion, the Pineapple in Dunmore, close to Edinburgh in Scotland, illustrates a similarly picturesque idea; it is shaped like a pineapple. It was commissioned in 1761 by John Murray (1730–1809), the fourth Earl of Dunmore, after his return from Virginia, where he served as the last British governor. In Dunmore, he cultivated pineapples in glass boxes alongside the wall to the left and right of the Pineapple; we can imagine this cultivation to have been similar to that of the figs and the vineyards on the palace hill of Sanssouci.

The medal of sublime folly, however, may be awarded to the garden Parque Nacional do Bucaco, which was crafted, starting in 1887 for the Portuguese King Charles I (1863–1908), next to the ruin of a small Carmelite monastery by the Italian theater architect Luigi Manini (1848–1936) in a neo-Manueline, wedding-cake style. Medieval Gothic elements combine with the exotic here, following in the footsteps of the English landscape garden in the United Kingdom. There, a turn to architecture's past was already evident in the 1720s and 1730s with designs for garden buildings that were later also published by the landscape and garden designer Batty Langley (1696–1751) in his *Ancient Architecture* (1741–1742). The Gothic Temple in Painshill (Surrey), a garden pavilion erected around 1745, was already aligned with those examples. Approximately at the same time, starting in 1741, the Gothic Temple (the Temple of Liberty) in Stowe, a significantly larger building, was created, which deliberately drew on the forms of the Gothic era. Its creator was James Gibbs (1682–1754), architect of St. Martin-in-the-Fields on Trafalgar Square in London, who was classically trained in Rome.

In Germany, the Gothic House in Wörlitz was among the first to reincorporate medieval elements. It was erected during the period from 1773 to 1813 in several construction phases based on designs by Friedrich Wilhelm von Erdmannsdorff (1736–1800) and Georg Christoph Hesekiel (1732–1818). Initially conceptualized as the gardener's residence, it was used from 1785 to 1813 as a private retreat by Leopold III Frederick Franz, Duke of Anhalt-Dessau (1740–1817), his wife in a morganatic marriage—the gardener's daughter, Luise Schoch—and their three children. The concept for the Gothic House was based on the English country estate of Sir Horace Walpole in Strawberry Hill, close to Twickenham in the Thames, which Duke Leopold III Frederick Franz had visited in 1764.

Consequently, garden architecture—especially the follies—became a testing ground for the art of building and construction. It embodied the variety of styles that emerged early in the eighteenth century and that were encouraged at the time. It is understandable that this novel trend was mainly approached on a smaller scale and not immediately used for expensive castles and residential palaces.

Left (from top):
Die schöne Sinesische Pagode vodr dem Stättlein Sinkicine in der Provinz Kantum gelegen *(The beautiful Chinese pagoda in front of the little town of Sinkicien in the province of Canton)*
Eine der Wundersamen Ketten-Brücken in Sina *(One of the amazing chain bridges in China)*
Sinesische Triumphbogen, deren eine Menge in der grossen Stätten zu sehen *(Chinese triumphal arch. Many of these can be seen in the large cities)*
Sinesische durch Kunst gemachte Lustberge und Höhlen mit Zimmern, Stieg, teichen, etc. *(Artificially created Chinese pleasure mountains, and caves with rooms, stairs, ponds, etc.)*
From Johann Bernhard Fischer von Erlach, Entwurff einer Historischen Architektur *(A Plan of Civil and Historical Architecture), 1721. Copperplate engravings.*

Below: Two half views of Chinese temples
From William Chambers, Traité des édifices, meubles, habits, machines, et ustensiles des Chinois. *(Treatise on the Buildings, Furniture, Habits, Machines, and Tools of the Chinese), 1776. Copperplate engraving.*

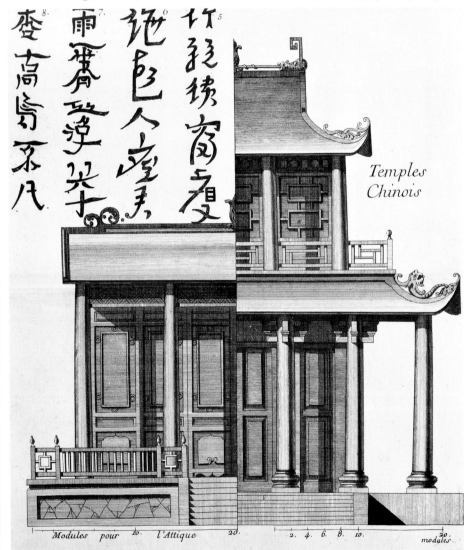

Chinese palace and pavilions in the park of Drottningholm Palace
Drottningholm-Stockholm, Sweden
Erected in 1753–1769 for Adolf Friedrich of Sweden from designs by Carl
Frederik Adelkrantz

Left: Ceiling with Chinese grotesque painting in the Gabinetto verso Levante alla China of the apartment of His Majesty in the Villa della Regina
Turin, Italy
From 1692, the property of Anne Marie d'Orléans, wife of Victor Amadeus II, Duke of Savoy.
Beginning of sophisticated interior decoration work, continued, after a change of ownership, in 1728 by her daughter, Maria Adelaide. Master plan of Filippo Juvara during this phase, with help from Giovanni Pietro Baroni di Travigliano, Pietro Massa, and his atelier.

Left and opposite: Chinese teahouse in the park of Sanssouci Palace
Potsdam, Germany
Built in 1754–1757 by Johann Gottfried Büring from sketches by King Frederick the Great of Prussia. The sculptures of the tea-drinking Chinese man and the string-instrument player by Johann Gottlieb Heymüller. Other sculptures by Johann Peter Benker.

Breakfast Pavilion and Baghdad Pavilion, Topkapi-Sarayl
Istanbul, Turkey
Seventeenth century

Turkish Pavilion, Chinese Pagoda, Temple
of Diana, and Chinese Bridge in the Parco
Durazzo Pallavicini
Genoa-Pegli, Italy
Built in 1840–1857 by the stage designer
Michele Canzio for Marchesa Clelia Durazzo

Mosque in the park of the Schwetzinger Schloss
Schwetzingen, Germany
Built by Nicolas de Pigage for Prince Elector Karl Theodor
of the Palatinate. On the eastern side of the park, a covered
walkway in the shape of a cloister surrounding a green
courtyard (1779–1784). On the western side, the main
mosque building with two minarets (1782–1786).

Left: View of the cupola of the mosque

Below: View of the courtyard with walkways

Right: The mosque with walkways

Opposite: Royal Pavilion
Brighton, England
Built in 1815–1822 by John Nash for George, Prince of Wales (Regent from 1811, later
King George IV). The exterior modeled on the Moghul palaces of India. Interior decoration
with reminiscences of China.

Below: Schloss auf den Pfaueninsel (Castle on Peacock Island)
Potsdam, Germany
King Friedrich Wilhelm II of Prussia bought the island that lay in one of the arms of the
Havel River in 1793 and had a summer residence there from 1794 to 1796, built by the court
master builder Johann Gottlieb Brendel.

The Turkish Tower in the park of Valtice Castle
Valtice, Czech Republic
Built in 1797–1802 by Joseph Hardtmuth for Prince Alois I von Liechtenstein
Left: View of the Turkish Tower
Below: Pencil drawing by Joseph Hardtmuth showing the first project for the Turkish Tower
with four flanking pavilions

Opposite left: Design for a Column of Trajan on Anninger Mountain near Mödling
Pen-and-pencil drawing with gray washed colors on paper by Joseph Hardtmuth,
construction director for Prince Johann I von Liechtenstein, 1811. The construction was
carried out in the same year, and the column collapsed immediately afterward.

Opposite right: Design for a "pyramid" on Anninger Mountain near Mödling, as a
substitute for the Column of Trajan
Pen-and-pencil drawing by Joseph Hardtmuth, construction director for Prince Johann I
von Liechtenstein, 1811

The Pineapple in Dunmore Park
Dunmore, Scotland
Built in 1761 by an unknown architect for John Murray,
fourth Earl of Dunmore

Below: The Watchmen's Tent in Haga Slott
Haga near Stockholm, Sweden
Built in 1787/1790 by Louis Jean Desprez for King Gustav III

Right: The Watchmen's Tent in Drottningholm Slott
Drottningholm-Stockholm, Sweden
Built in 1781/82 by Carl Frederik Adelkrantz and Louis Jean Desprez for King Gustav III

Left and right: Monopteros in Parco Querini
Vicenza, Italy
Originally the park of the Palazzo Capra-Querini.
It was surrounded by the Venetian Gothic city
walls and the Bacchiglione and Astichello
Rivers. Its focal point is the tiny island with the
Monopteros by Antonio Piovene, 1820.

Below: Labyrinth in the park of the Villa Pisani
Stra, Italy
Nine concentric circles formed by boxwood hedges
surround an orientation-and-observation tower
and a statue of Minerva, 1720/21.

Left: Fasanenschlösschen (Pheasant Manor)
Moritzburg, Germany
Built in 1769–1782 by Johann Daniel Schade and Johann Gottlieb Hauptmann for
Prince Elector Friedrich August III. In 1776 the jetty, the lighthouse, the harbor, and the
Dardanelles wall were added at the lake.

Below: Schloss Favorite
Ludwigsburg, Germany
Built in 1717–1723 by court architect Donato Giuseppe Frisoni for Duke Eberhard Ludwig

Temple of Apollo in the park of the Schwetzinger Schloss
Schwetzingen, Germany
Built on an artificial rock formation in 1762–1775 by Nicolas de Pigage for Prince
Elector Karl Theodor of the Palatinate. Sculptures by Peter Anton von Verschaffelt, 1773.

Right and below: Belvedere in the park of the Villa Pisani
Stra, Italy
Built in 1720 by Girolamo Frigimelica de` Roberti for Alvise and Almorò Pisani

Opposite above: Haus der Laune (House of the Good Mood) in the park of Schloss Laxenburg
Laxenburg-Vienna, Austria
Built before 1798 by Johann Ferdinand Hetzendorf von Hohenberg for Maria Theresa

Left: Design for the furnishing of the music room

Right: Haus der Laune in the imperial pleasure garden at Laxenburg. Study for the edition of engravings of Laurenz Janscha, ca. 1800.

Opposite below: Dove House in the park of Schönbrunn Palace
Vienna-Hietzing, Austria
Built in 1772–1780 by Johann Ferdinand Hetzendorf von Hohenberg for Maria Theresa

Below: Design for one of the small fishermen's houses of the fishing village in the park of Schloss Laxenburg
Laxenburg-Vienna, Austria
Created by order of the second wife of Emperor Franz I of Hapsburg, Maria Theresa of Naples-Sicily. Watercolors by unknown painter, ca. 1798.

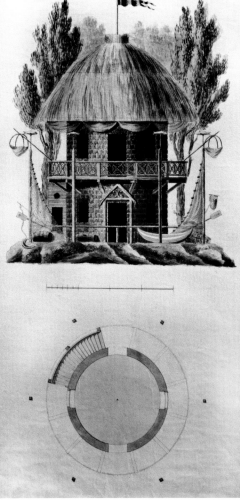

Opposite, left above: View from the Cobenzl toward Vienna (Austria)
After the abolition of the Jesuit Order, transformation of the Jesuit houses on the Reisenberg into a castle, planting of a spacious garden, and establishment of a publicly accessible inn by Count Johann Philipp Cobenzl in 1773. Watercolor over pencil by Laurenz Janscha, ca. 1796.

Opposite, left middle: The Gothic Temple on the Predigtstuhl estate of Prince Gallitzin, near Vienna
Acquisition of extensive properties on the Predigtstuhl hill by the Russian ambassador in Vienna, Demetrius Michailovich Gallitzin. From 1785, construction of the castle and the installation of a spacious landscaped garden containing artificial Roman ruins and two round temples, one in a Gothic style and one in an antiquity style. Watercolor over pencil by Laurenz Janscha, ca. 1790.

Opposite, left below: The Little Dutch Village (Hameau) in Neuwaldegg near Vienna
Acquisition of the Neuwaldegg estate in 1765 by Field Marshal Franz Moritz von Lacy. Subsequent installation of an English garden (completed in 1796) and a village with seventeen simple huts at the summit, to serve as accommodations for Lacy's guests. Watercolor over pencil by Laurenz Janscha, ca. 1790.

Opposite right: Two views of the Rosenbaum Garden in Vienna, Austria Architectural designs by Josef Kornhäusel for Josef Karl Rosenbaum. Rosenbaum was employed by the Esterházy family but had to leave their service after his marriage. In 1816 he installed his garden (extensive alterations in 1826), and it became a center of Viennese society life. Colored outline etching by Eduard Gurk, ca. 1820.

Opposite and below bottom: Doric column (La Colonne, 1781) and Pyramid in the Désert de Retz
Chambourcy, France
Constructed in 1774 by Nicolas François Barbier for François Henry Racine de Monville

Below left: Star Pyramid in the cemetery at Stirling
Stirling, Scotland
In 1863, next to the old Valley Cemetery, with the graves of artisans, Drummond's Pleasure Ground was laid out. The monumental pyramid was erected as a memorial to the heroes and martyrs of Presbyterianism by William Barclay on commission from William Drummond.

Below middle: Pyramid in the Parc Monceau
Paris, France
Inauguration of the first gardens of Louis-Phillippe-Joseph, Duke of Orléans and Chartres, designed in 1769 by Louis Carmontelle.. Transformed into an English landscaped park from 1785 to 1788, by the Scottish garden designer Thomas Blaikie. Construction of numerous small architectural features.

Below right: Pyramid at the Marble Palace in the New Garden
Potsdam, Germany
Constructed in 1791/92 by Andreas Krüger and Carl Gotthard Langhans for King Frederick the Great of Prussia

Left and below: Prittlach Obelisk
Lednice, Czech Republic
Constructed in 1797/98 by Josef Hardtmuth

Below: Obeslisk in the park at Chiswick
Chiswick-London, England
Constructed in 1729 by Sir Wiliam Kent

Obelisk to honor Gideon von Laudon (below) and the Victory Column (right) in the park of Ernstbrunn Castle, Austria. Castle park restored in 1775 by Emmanuel Joseph von Herigoyen and Benedikt Henrici. Engraving by Johann Andreas Ziegler, end of the eighteenth century. Watercolor by Laurenz Janscha, 1797.

Below right: The Waterfall and Obelisk in the imperial garden at Schönbrunn Vienna-Hietzing, Austria Constructed in 1777 by Johann Ferdinand Hetzendorf von Hohenberg. Colored outline etching by Laurenz Janscha, after a sketch of Johann Andreas Ziegler, 1785.

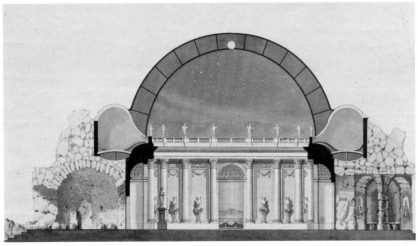

Park at Schönau Castle
Schönau an der Triesting, Austria.
Castle redesigned in 1797 by Baron
von Braun and surrounded by a
landscaped park. In the center of the
park lies the Grotto Mountain built
after sketches by Johann Ferdinand
Hetzendorf von Hohenberg.

Left above: The Grotto Mountain of
Count Fries in Vöslau near Vienna.
Copperplate engraving by Carl Schütz,
1777.

Far left: Section drawing of the Temple
of Night. Pencil-and-ink drawing
with gray washed colors by Johann
Ferdinand Hetzendorf von Hohenberg,
ca. 1800.

Left: The Temple of Night in the garden
of Baron von Braun in Schönau.
Colored aquatint by Benedikt Piringer,
ca. 1820.

Ruins in the garden of Schönbrunn Palace
Vienna-Hietzing, Austria
Constructed in 1777 by Johann Ferdinand Hetzendorf von Hohenberg. Colored outline etching by
Laurenz Janscha after a sketch of Johann Andreas Ziegler, 1785.

Below: Grotto with a Doric column portico
Moscow, Russia
Built in 1821 by Osip Beauvais for Czar Alexander I at the foot of the middle
arsenal tower (Venetian architect Alovisio Novo, 1495) on the Kremlin Wall

Right: Ensemble of ancient spolia and remnants in the castle park of Klein-Glienecke
Berlin-Zehlendorf, Germany
Installed after 1822 by Karl Friedrich Schinkel, Ludwig Persius, and Peter Joseph
Lenné for Prince Carl of Prussia

PALACES WITHOUT WALLS

Orangeries and Greenhouses

The idea of the orangerie and the greenhouse is inseparably linked with the triumphal success of Italian and French garden design. Citrus trees—especially lemon trees—played a central role in these gardens. The construction of such a prestigious garden would have been unthinkable without them. In earlier gardens the main focus was on plants, purely for reasons of design. Later interest focused on fruits and on the citrus plants in all their great and largely unfamiliar variety. These plants became a commodity much in demand by growers, collectors, and merchants.

Such plants possessed only one major disadvantage: They were sensitive to the cold. Even in southern latitudes—in Rome, in Tuscany, in northern Italy, and certainly anywhere farther north—they needed protection from the winter. They could survive temperatures in the upper 20s and even a small amount of snow. They had to be protected from very low temperatures, however, and taken into protected areas.

Initially, provisional solutions were attempted in Italy. One very early invention was the *limonaia* (lemon greenhouse), named for the most popular fruit tree that it housed. It was a building completely exposed to the sun. Its large window surfaces were covered with mats at night and during periods of extreme cold. The windows were simply unhinged during the summer so that the sunshine needed for ripening could flow in unhindered. A process of "fortification" gradually took place. The huge glass surfaces remained transparent, but they were protected by shutters that could be opened or closed to provide additional protection from the cold.

On Lake Garda the famous lemon orchards with their large juicy fruit determined the agricultural landscape until the 1970s. Here, light, tall buildings with granite columns and wooden coverings were used. These buildings lent a characteristic and varied appearance to entire regions whether the structures were furnished with glass or completely open in the summer.

In Tuscany, Grand Duke Leopold I of Hapsburg-Lothringen (1747–1792) ensured that the Boboli Gardens in Florence received their first large, impressive *limonaia* in 1785. The development of the gardens of the Villa Pisani, near Venice, from a small Baroque park to the impressive monumental construction of the late eighteenth and early nineteenth centuries, can still be viewed with wonder today. In the winter only the wooden shutters are normally opened during the day; in warm weather the glass windows are opened wide; at dusk, both are closed tightly. The air in the *limonaia* is additionally warmed by small heaters, but only on the coldest winter days. The charm of this architecture lies in its ephemeral character and in its changeability. Its appearance can alter completely, depending on the climatic situation. The plants themselves are raised and tended in ideal conditions. They need the cold temperatures of winter in order not to bud too early and to prevent pest infestation.

Garden enthusiasts had already been forced to search for appropriate and more "professional" solutions near the raw climate north of the Alps. They began by planting lemon trees, vines, and figs next to walls. In the winter these would be covered and sheltered by additional temporary structures. Duke Christoph of Württemberg (1515–1568) constructed the first orangerie built according to this model at his Residenz in Stuttgart. Here, the orange tree was introduced to the German garden, alongside the lemon tree. At about the same time in England, Sir Francis Carew (ca. 1530–1611) succeeded in cultivating orange saplings for the first time at his estate Beddington, near London.

The citrus fruit had also been discovered in France in the late fifteenth century. In a letter to his brother, King Charles VIII (1470–1498) waxes enthusiastic about the "hesperidian fragrances" and the "beautiful gardens that I have in this city. . . . It seems to me that all I need is Adam and Eve in order to make it into an earthly paradise." He introduced citrus fruits to his castle at Blois in 1495. While visiting Blois in 1517 the Cardinal of Aragon admired the artfully designed garden beds that Pacello de Mercogliano (ca. 1455–1534), a priest and garden designer from Naples, had created for King Charles VIII. The cardinal particularly mentioned "the many lemon trees and large orange trees contained in wooden boxes." When King Francis I (1494–1547) confiscated the estates of Duke Charles de Bourbon in 1522, he took all of the Seville orange trees, cultivated at great expense by the duke on his estates, and had them transported to his own park at Fontainebleau.

The interior of these early greenhouses were warmed by coal basins. This method of heating was also used in homes in Italy. Cracks or splits in the basin were stopped with straw or tow. Johann Wolfgang von Goethe gives a dramatic description of this method in his *Italienische Reise* (Italian Journey), written between 1813 and 1817. Soon the first terrace gardens were laid out. During the construction of the Château d'Anet, designed by the architect Philiberte de l'Orme for Diane de Poitiers, mistress of King Henry II (1519–1559), an arcade passageway was built alongside the terrace. The citrus trees could be placed in the passageway during the winter.

At Versailles, from 1768 and onward, the greenhouses constituted a palace with its own character, thanks to Jules Hardouin-Mansart's ambitious expansion of the orangerie. Here, laurels, myrtles, and pomegranates spent the winter alongside citrus trees. A hall 1,200 feet in length, bordered by Tuscan columns and closed off by double French windows, stretched out between the lateral walls. In this hall temperatures could be maintained so constant that no further heating was necessary. Today the full splendor of the giant and often extremely old plants can unfold in the parterre that lies in front of the hall.

With its introduction to Versailles the orangerie had become a permanent feature of castle architecture. Augustin-Charles d'Aviler (1653–1701) devoted an entire chapter to it in his book *Cours d'architecture* (Course in Architecture) that appeared in 1691: "Since the orange tree is one of the most beautiful adornments of a garden, with its blossoms, its fruit, its fragrance, and its leaves that remain green even in winter, people strive to cultivate it carefully. They build greenhouses, called orangeries, where they can walk around as in a gallery, even in winter. The[se orangeries] can be found in every large garden. The glass windows must face southward, and both inner and outer windows must be firmly closed in winter."

Whatever was thought good for the great gardens of France was acceptable for Austrian castle and garden architecture as well. Imperial vice-chancellor Duke Friedrich Karl von Schönborn (1674–1746) had Johann Lukas von Hildebrandt (1668–1745) build an extensive Baroque garden palace between 1711 and 1715 near Göllersdorf in Lower Austria, north of Vienna. The palace had a splendidly furnished orangerie, of course. The frescoes by Jonas Drentwett (1650–1720) on the walls of the orangerie still, in part, display remarkably fresh color. They also testify to the richness and significance granted to rooms that were used not only for storing plants but for taking pleasurable strolls during the cold seasons.

During the construction in Vienna of the Belvedere, the summer palace of Prince Eugen Franz of Savoy-Carignan (1663–1736), a Pomeranzenhaus (Seville-orange house) that was notable for its refined design was built between 1717 and 1719. Here, too, the building consisted essentially of two lateral walls and a longitudinal wall that joined them and served as the rear wall of the building. This wall was adorned with sculptures and was architecturally richly ordered. Salomon Kleiner (1700–1761) published between 1731 and 1740 an oeuvre of engravings called *Wunder würdiges Kriegs- und Siegs-Lager des unvergleichlichen Helden unserer Zeit. Oder Eigentliche Vor und Abbildungen der Hoff- Lust- und Garten Gebaüde des Durchlauchtigsten Fürstens und Herrn Eugenii Francisci zu Savoyen und Piemont* (Wondrous War and Victory Camp of the Incomparable Hero of Our Time. Or the Actual Representations and Images of the Palace, Summer House, and Garden of the Most Serene Lord Eugen Franz of Savoy and Piedmont). Kleiner included three images of this architectural jewel: the ground plan, *Das Pommeranzen Haus, wie solches im Sommer anzusehen ist* (The Seville-orange house as seen in summer), and finally the *Prospekt des obigen Pommeranzen Hauses, wie es im Herbst zugedecket und im Frühling wiederum abgedecket ist* (View of the above-mentioned Seville-orange house, covered over in the autumn and uncovered again in the spring). In these images we possess wonderful examples of an architecture that combines functionality with a sort of charming variability. At the Belvedere there is also a permanent greenhouse constructed entirely of wood that Kleiner displays in his *View of the Large Greenhouse*.

In Potsdam, greenhouses lend character to an entire castle. The Weinbergterrassen (vineyard terraces) were laid out in front of the south facade of Sanssouci Palace from August 10, 1744 to 1746 by command of King Friedrich of Prussia (1712–1786). These terraces give the garden its distinctive character by incorporating a series of 196 strictly structured glass niches. The garden's appearance changes with the seasons: the luxuriant green of the vines and fig trees in the summer, the brilliant yellow of the autumnal vine foliage—closed up and glassed in during the winter, open and free in the summer. The Great Vine, a huge grape vine planted in 1768, is still one of the biggest attractions at Hampton Court Palace in London.

The greenhouses that the English architect and gardener Joseph Paxton (1803–1865) designed were elegant and ingenious. They are distinguished by a very economical use of materials and great delicacy in their construction. They are considered forerunners of modern architecture on account of their functionality and architectural clarity. This trend toward modernity was highlighted at Chatsworth House in Derbyshire by Paxton's Great Conservatory of 1836 (no longer extant), and the Glass Wall, a connecting passageway of 1848. The most famous example of Paxton's inchoate modernity is his Crystal Palace—still constructed using wood—for the World Exhibition of 1851 in Hyde Park, London. His creations were the forerunners of the iron and steel buildings that would shortly dominate civil engineering for many years, becoming ever more elegant and sophisticated in the process.

The breathtaking development in the direction of large greenhouses opened up new possibilities for their use. The goal was no longer the temporary protection of small lemon and orange trees but giant palm trees and other exotic plants from the tropics. Such plants were acquired during the first half of the nineteenth century in the course of often expensive expeditions and brought back to Europe where they were carefully bred and propagated in greenhouses. New plants had new requirements. Instead of moderate temperature settings just a few degrees above freezing, the new tropical greenhouses required very different conditions. The problems to be solved were not matters of construction but of thermics and building physics. Remarkable buildings were soon erected, bringing a new chapter to the history of architecture. Greenhouses were no longer viewed as places for plants to be stored and to spend the winter, but rather as rooms, often directly connected with the residence, where people could meet and converse. The Palm House of Bicton Park in Devonshire, built in the 1820s, is a very early example of this sort of greenhouse. A somewhat later example is the one at the Castle of Lednice, a town that lies in the Czech Republic near the Austrian border. The greenhouse was built from 1843 to 1845 by Georg Wingelmüller (1810–1848) according to plans of Peter Hubert Desvignes (1804–1883).

Developments accelerated toward the middle of the nineteenth century. Everything seemed possible. Buildings became ever larger and more elegant and were soon used for exhibitions as well. The Wilhelma (1842–1846), a park in Stuttgart, was built according to plans of Karl Ludwig van Zanth (1796–1857). It integrated the activities of life and the accommodation of plants in a most elegant way. The historicism that optically dominates in the Wilhelma recedes in gardens constructed later, in favor of strict engineering constructions. The Palm House in Kew Gardens, built by the foundryman Richard Turner in the 1840s, according to plans of Decimus Burton (1800–1881), is perhaps the purest of these engineering constructions. It is free of any unnecessary adornment that could blur its lines; here, "form follows function." Toward the end of the nineteenth century the appearance of greenhouses once more became somewhat less individual. The Temperate House in Kew Gardens, again built according to plans of Decimus Burton, or the Palmenhaus (Palm House), built by Ignaz Gridl and Sigmund Wagner in Vienna-Schönbrunn (opened in 1882) according to the plans of the Imperial Court Architect Xaver von Segenschmid (1839–1888), no longer possessed the crystalline clarity of this type of building manifested in its first great masterpieces.

Left: Lemon from the Lake Garda region in Italy

Below: Limonaia
Gargano, Italy

Right: Limonaia of a country house
Villa Lagarina near Rovereto, Italy
Built in the nineteenth century. The glass panes are completely
removed in the spring. During the warm seasons only the
supporting structure remains.

Left and right: Greenhouses at Villa Pisani Stra, Italy
Built in the eighteenth and nineteenth centuries. Famed for breeding the most varied types of citrus plants. The fascination of early greenhouses is due to the change in their appearance, depending on whether they are closed or open.

Above: Malus Citria *(Citron),* Malus Limonia *(Lemon), winter apple. Colored copperplate engraving from Johann Wilhelm Weinmann,* Phytanthoza iconographia oder eigentliche Vorstellung etliche Tausend … aus aller Welt-Theilen gesammelter Pflantzen, Bäume, Stauden, Kräuter *(Phytanthoza Iconographia or Actual Representation of Many Thousand … Plants, Trees, Perennials, and Herbs Collected from All Parts of the World), 1737–1743.*

Above: Greenhouse (Conservative Wall) or Portland Walk in the park of Chatsworth House
Chatsworth, England
Constructed by Joseph Paxton in 1842. Originally a supporting structure with panels made of blue-and-white-striped linen curtains. These were replaced with glass panels by John Robertson in 1850.

Right: Palm House of the Wörlitz Garden Realm
Wörlitz, Germany
Erected in 1777–1779

Left: Greenhouse in the park of Telč Castle
Telč, Czech Republic
Built in the second quarter of the nineteenth
century for Count Alois Arnošt Podstatzky-
Liechtenstein Kastelkorn and his wife, Amalia
von Clary und Aldringen

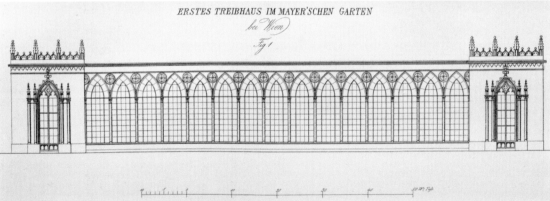

ERSTES TREIBHAUS IM MAYER'SCHEN GARTEN
bei Wien
Fig 1

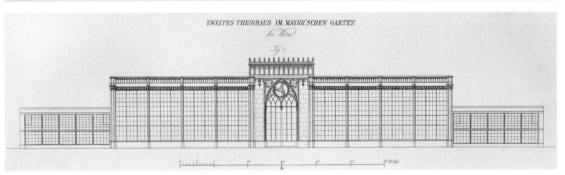

ZWEITES TREIBHAUS IM MAYER'SCHEN GARTEN
bei Wien
Fig 1

Left: First and second greenhouses in the
Mayer'schen Garden
Vienna-Penzing, Austria
Designs by Pietro Nobile, 1838

Right: Greenhouse in the garden on the
Burgberg
Graz, Austria
Constructed in 1842/43

The winter garden of Lednice Castle
Lednice, Czech Republic
Built in 1843–1845 for Prince Alois II von Liechtenstein
by George Wingelmüller after designs by Hubert Desvignes.
Directly accessible from the salon of the neo-Gothic castle.

*Left: View of the winter garden of Lednice Castle.
Watercolor by Rudolf von Alt, 1842.*

*Below left: View of the interior with cast-iron columns
imitating bamboo*

*Below: Page with eggplants. From Hortus Botanicus.
Watercolor with gouache by Ferdinand, Franz, and
Joseph Bauer, 1777–1804.*

*Right: View of the end of the greenhouse, in the form of a
half cupola*

Wilhelma Palace. Garden house with residence and greenhouses in Moorish style
Stuttgart, Germany
Built in 1837–1842 by Karl Ludwig Zanth for King Wilhelm I

313

Palm House in the Royal Botanic Gardens at Kew
Kew-Richmond, England
Constructed by Decimus Burton and Richard
Turner for Queen Victoria. Opened in early 1848.

Palm House in the park at Schönbrunn Palace
Vienna-Hietzing, Austria
Built in 1880–1882 by Franz von Segenschmid for Emperor Franz Joseph I

THE ART OF FUNCTIONAL BEAUTY

Trellises, Gazebos, and Pergolas

The most direct interpenetration of architecture and nature probably occurs in trellises, gazebos, and pergolas. On the one hand, there is the architectural construct, most often made from wooden slats or stone-wall parts, later joined together with iron; and on the other hand, there is the vegetation that intimately connects with these elements and is capable of destroying them with its force—as often happens in the case of wisteria. Walls are sometimes completely encased with uninhibited overgrowth of greenery, and architectural structures are created, such as pavilions that are exclusively characterized by this latticework—or arcades, where both elements symbiotically complement each other.

Such trellises already existed in antiquity: Roman murals are a reliable source attesting to the sophistication and wealth that Hellenistic and Roman garden culture had already developed. Trellises blossomed anew during the Renaissance and especially during the Baroque period: They made "cultivated" garden rooms and pavilions possible. These easy-to-erect latticeworks, with their characteristic vegetation, were found in the monumental parks of nobility and royalty as well as in smaller bourgeois gardens—not least because of limited financial means.

Aside from large palaces and their parks, some of the most monumental works are the *Geleiteten Linden* (guided linden trees) in Germany, where nature and the work of man grew together into monumental formations. Maybe the most artistic of these constructs was the *Grosse Linde* (big linden tree) of Peesten in Franconia, which collapsed and was removed in 1947 after a long period of neglect and was then reestablished in 2001. In the center, a linden tree was shaped into an almost cubical dance house; one could reach the dance room on the second floor through a stone spiral staircase. The dance floor—two hundred people could be seated there for a banquet—was propped up by the trunk itself and twelve wooden supports (mentioned in 1657); since 1770 by stone supports and the stone spiral staircase, erected that same year. From the second floor, one could look out of the windows onto the surrounding area.

Without doubt, the art of treillage reached its peak in the parks of the Palace of Versailles, which in the Bosquet de l'Encelade in particular—a trellis that was later lost, but reconstructed at the end of the twentieth century—displays every design possibility at the junction of man's work and nature. In the gardens of Hampton Court (England) and Het Loo (the Netherlands)—both of them recently restored—of Schwetzingen (Germany) and of Schönbrunn (Austria), trellises, gazebos, and pergolas also played a central role. In Schönbrunn, trellis pavilions with arcades in between demarcated the Kammergarten and the Kronprinzengarten as private areas of the palace park. The architecture of these pavilions made out of fine latticework painted white and green later appeared in the Grünes Lusthaus, or Dianatempel, erected in 1755 for Maria Theresa in the palace garden of Laxenburg. Interestingly, the inside of the pavilion, which is also made entirely of wood, is decorated to this day with a ceiling painting applied on plaster. These pavilions always required intensive care. Every few years, new paint had to be applied, and rotted wood had to be replaced with new wood at more frequent intervals. In Schwetzingen, many of those structures were therefore made out of iron early on. The same happened in the garden of Sanssouci in Potsdam, where the palace's lateral pavilions and its front arcade—originally nail works erected according to plans by Georg Wenzelslaus von Knobelsdorff (1699–1753)—were transformed into iron constructs in 1770.

Many of these trellises were neglected during the rise of the English garden and subsequently disappeared entirely. At the same time, the influence of antiquity led to a completely new understanding of the close interconnection between architecture and plant growth. Karl Friedrich Schinkel (1781–1841) and his student Ludwig Persius (1803–1845) extensively explored this subject in their parks for the Prussian royalty. With their pergolas at the Glienicke Palace, at the Gärtnerhaus (Gardener's House), and at the Römische Bäder (Roman Baths), as well as at Charlottenhof Palace, they intentionally implemented the pergola theme in order to transmit a feeling of bucolic Italian country life—for example, the atmosphere of estates in the Roman Campagna—in the faraway cities of Berlin and Potsdam. In the garden of Hermann von Pückler-Muskau (1785–1871) in Branice, the constructions of the Monument for Henriette Sonntag (after 1845) achieved an elegance hitherto unknown, because of the new, slim material of iron—the composed colorfulness of the painted iron played a significant role in this. The same can be said of the iron gazebos and arcatures in the palace park of Kroměříž in Moravia, which were also built shortly before 1850 by Bishop Maximilian Joseph Gottfried of Sommerau Beeckh (1769–1853) in the course of the redesign of the originally Baroque park into a spacious landscape garden.

A major shift did not occur until the end of the nineteenth century, particularly in the twentieth century, with the arrival of historicism, art nouveau, and art deco, which rediscovered these elements for private as well as public gardens. During this period, very ambitious examples of such constructs were created that, in most cases, have survived to this day.

The delightful garden of the Castle of Miramare, close to Trieste, designed by the court gardener Josef Laube from Laxenburg and his successor, Anton Jelinek, in the last quarter of the nineteenth century for Archduke Ferdinand Maximilian of Austria (1832–1867), later the unlucky Emperor Maximilian of Mexico, had a whole system of such pergolas, in the center of which lay a plaza covered with wisteria. The wood is painted bloodred here, and many copies of ancient bronzes have been placed inside of and around the pergolas in an attempt to once more simulate the appearance of villa gardens of antiquity.

In the Friedrichsplatz around the water tower in Mannheim, the pergola is an elaborate example of the waning trend of historicism with stone columns and cast-bronze lanterns that shape the appearance of the decorative inner-city square, created from 1899 to 1903 according to designs by the Berlin architect Bruno Schmitz (1858–1916). The pergola at the entrance to the rose garden of the Parc de la Grange in Geneva is entwined with roses and has a much cooler effect. Besides the bronze sculptures that the pergola shelters—conveying a quality of romanticism—it is also characterized by great coolness and dispassion.

Pergola in front of the Gardener's House
Potsdam, Germany
Built in 1829/1830 by Karl Friedrich Schinkel and construction
supervisor Ludwig Persius

Trellis Pavilions with arcades on both sides of Schönbrunn Palace
Vienna-Hietzing, Austria
Constructed in the eighteenth century. Altered several times, particularly
in the area of the Crown Prince Garden. Partially redesigned.

Left and below: Iron trellises and pavilions at Sanssouci Palace
Potsdam, Germany
Trellises constructed of wooden slats and nailed together were replaced in 1770 by iron construction according to designs by Georg Wenzeslaus von Knobelsdorff.

Right: Green summerhouse (Temple of Diana) in the park of Laxenburg Palace
Laxenburg-Vienna, Austria
Erected after 1755 for Empress Maria Theresa as the center of a planned zoo

Trellises made of simple wooden slats at the Petit Trianon
Versailles, France
Constructed in 1764–1768 by Ange-Jacques Gabriel

Left: Arcade with flowering wisteria in the Parque Nacional do Buçaco
Mata do Buçaco, Portugal
Built ca. 1890

Below left: Pergola at the entrance to the rose garden of the Parc de la Grange
Geneva, Switzerland
Erected for William Favre at the beginning of the twentieth century.
Donated to the city of Geneva in 1917.

Below: Pergola in the garden of Villa Ephrussi de Rothschild on Cap Ferrat
Saint-Jean-Cap-Ferrat, France
Villa built in 1907–1912 for Béatrice de Rothschild and her husband, Maurice Ephrussi

Right: Trellises in the park of the Castello di Miramare
Miramare near Trieste, Italy
Constructed in the third quarter of the nineteenth century by Josef Laube and Anton Jelinek for Archduke Ferdinand Maximillian of Austria

328

Below: Monument for Henriette Sonntag in the Branitzer Park
Cottbus, Germany
Built in 1845 by Hermann von Pückler-Muskau

Opposite: Josef Höger, Blick aus einem Gartenpavillon auf das Palais Rasumovsky in Wien-Erdberg (View from a Garden Pavilion Toward the Palais Rasumovsky in Vienna-Erdberg). Watercolor, after 1837. Palace built in 1806/07 by Louis Montoyer for Andrea Kirillovich Rasumovsky. Garden redesigned in 1837 for Prince Alois II von Liechtenstein.

Left: Trellises in the park of the Château de Beloeil
Beloeil, Belgium
The Château de Beloeil, the estate of the Princes of Ligne, is considered to be the Belgian Versailles. The eighteenth-century
park was expanded by the addition of English gardens in the nineteenth century.

Below: Simple arbor in the park of the Archiepiscopal Palace at Kroměříž
Kroměříž, Czech Republic
Transformation of the original Baroque park into a spacious landscaped garden with numerous architectural features
shortly before 1850 by Bishop Maximillian Joseph Gottfried von Sommerau Beeckh

THE ART OF BEAUTIFUL CUTTING

Topiary

Only few elements in garden design became more popular than *topiaries*, as plants that have been cut into shapes are called. The term can be traced back to Pliny the Elder (23–79 A.D.), who described the art of tree and hedge cutting as *opus topiarium*. In ancient Rome, gardeners were called *topiarii*. These topiaries range from entire hedges and garden circumvallations, which almost flow around the gardens with contours cut in an organically soft manner, to playful boxwood pyramids or boxwood spheres that adorn a front yard, to the occasional green wall in an austerely stereometric shape that conveys architectural severity.

The desire to create architectural elements by means of cutting bushes and trees must always have been present in human history. Already during the Renaissance, examples from antiquity were invoked—particularly the *Historia naturalis*, published circa 77 A.D. by Pliny the Elder—and hedges crowned with sculptures were set up instead of walls. In his work *Hypnerotomachia Poliphili* (1499), Francesco Colonna portrays Cythera, the Island of Love, with its hedges and other groups of plants trimmed in the shape of figures in triumphal marches and battles. Here, plants that had been cut into decorative shapes were also depicted for the first time. Already during the Renaissance, entire walls and facades had been designed in this manner, and they even imitated doorways and windows with openings.

In his work *Liber ruralium commodorum*, first published in 1471 in Augsburg, Pietro de' Crescenzi (ca. 1230/35–ca. 1320) describes the erection of a house made only of trees cut into shape: "All surfaces, the hallways, and the chambers should be measured and designated, and instead of walls, trees should be planted; fruit trees, if desired, that grow easily, such as cherries and apples, or even better, willows, white poplars, and elm trees should be planted, and by means of grafting, as well as with the aid of stakes, slats, and ribbons, they will grow for several years until they form the walls and the roof."

In England, in 1625, already intensive polemics had arisen against this formative pruning. It probably targeted the plentiful topiaries in Hampton Court, which had been established there under the government of Henry VIII (1491–1547). In his essay "On Gardens" of 1625, Francis Bacon (1561–1626) wrote about the images cut into juniper or other garden materials: "That is for children." Bacon recommended simpler architectural shapes. The French garden theoretician Antoine-Joseph Dezallier d'Argenville (1680–1765) codified these shapes in his *La théorie et la pratique du jardinage* of 1709 and delivered crucial models with his engravings. In Germany, these were provided by Matthias Diesel (1675–1752), who presented topiaries composed of stereometric formations in his work *Erlustierende Augenweide in Vorstellung herrlicher Garten- und Lustgebäude* of 1717. Interestingly, such models were also created out of stone for the fence posts of the Bavarian castle of Seehof.

The idea to shape perfect architecture out of and with greenery reached its peak in the Baroque garden. The structure of parterres and boscages could be understood as a series of rooms, with the parterres forming the free spaces and the green hedges of the boscages constituting the inner rooms—the *salle*, *cabinet*, and *gallerie*—with the sky as the ceiling. This can be compared with the interior design of the day: a similar garden conceit appears in the *Bergl-Zimmer* rooms of Schönbrunn Palace near Vienna, named after the painter of the frescoes, Johann Wenzel Bergl (1718–1789). Here, the walls are covered with a wild jungle of tropical plants, which support the ceiling—designed as a view of the sky. Plants are understood and used as architecturally supporting elements. In his *De la distribution des maisons de plaisance* of 1737, Jacques-François Blondel (1705–1774) describes a round hall, "whose four walls are niches designed to accommodate buffets. On the inside, facades out of hornbeam arches have been erected, and behind those arches, a balustrade out of the same material has been installed. There are no carpets of grass in this room, because it is intended to be used for balls; its rural decoration facilitates pleasant illumination during festivities at night." The inner room and the open space outside follow the same design principles and become almost interchangeable.

The design of garden rooms and green walls was most fully realized at Versailles, particularly in the areas around the Grand Trianon, where a wide range of layout geometry and derived complex typological design were developed. With the arrival of the English garden, and the accompanying contempt for and subsequent destruction of all geometric schemes, many of the ground-plan systems were neglected, changed, or even destroyed. Here, the restoration and reconstruction efforts of the past few centuries have managed to re-create much of the glory of these parks, which had disappeared or was no longer evident. In the course of such measures, many topiary gardens were also restored or entirely re-created; for example, the garden of the Château de Marqueyssac in Vézac (Aquitaine, France) and the garden of Levens Hall (South Cumbria, England).

The park of Levens Hall was originally created, starting in 1694, by the French gardener Guillaume Beaumont, a student of André Le Nôtre in Versailles, with boxwood pruned in a strictly geometrical or an amorphous manner. Many changes were later made to this garden, which has always been well groomed; and these modifications contributed greatly to the picturesque appearance it has today. Especially during the late nineteenth and early twentieth centuries, topiaries made of individual boxwood plants or out of multiple boxwood plants joined together in hedges were very popular.

The garden of the Château de Marqueyssac in the French region of Dordogne was also created during this time. Palace and garden rise high above the valley of the river with the same name and offer a wonderful view of the surrounding scenery with other picturesque castles. Starting in 1861, the old estate was completely renovated under the new owner, Julien de Cerval. Particularly, the garden experienced a drastic redesign, which is still being continued under its current owner, the organization Kleber Rossillon. The garden possesses a lightness and liveliness that is unusual for historic parks. Today, there are more than 150,000 trimmed boxwood plants, cypresses, and linden trees that have turned it into a major crowd-pleasing attraction.

Boxwood plants in the Jardines de Sabatini at the foot of the Palacio Real
Madrid, Spain
Initial creation of garden followed the demolition of the royal stables in 1933.
Opened by King Juan Carlos I in 1978.

337

Left: An avenue of small citrus trees on the shore
of the Isola Bella in the Lago Maggiore
Stresa, Italy
Created in 1632 by Antonio Crivelli for
Carlo III Borromeo and his wife, Isabella
d'Adda

Right: Garden with cypresses and boxwoods
trimmed in the shape of spheres
Amboise, France
Laid out at the end of the twentieth century
on the site of the first Renaissance garden in
France. The original garden was laid out in
1495 by the Neapolitan architect Dom Pacello
da Mercogliano for King Charles VIII.

Conically trimmed hornbeams and boxwoods seen in the change of the seasons

Below top and right: Front garden of the Riddarhuset in Gamla stan (the Assembly House of the Swedish nobility)
Stockholm, Sweden
Built in 1671–1674 by Simon de la Vallée

Below bottom: Forecourt of the Royal Palace
Stockholm, Sweden
Built by Jean de la Vallée (from 1651), Nicodemus Tessin the Elder (from 1666), and Nicodemus Tessin the Younger (from 1692) for King Gustavus Adolphus II and his daughter, Christine of Sweden. After the fire of 1667, further modernization measures by King Charles XII and King Gustav III.

Gardens of the Generalife Palace with the Alhambra in the background
Granada, Spain
Restoration in 1931. Completed by Francisco Prieto Moreno in 1951.

Boxwoods in the topiary garden
Levens Hall, England
Residence of the Bellingham family from the 1590s. Since 1688, the property of
Colonel James Graham. Garden created in 1694 by Guillaume Beaumont, a disciple
of André Le Nôtre at Versailles.

Boxwoods in the garden of the Château de Marqueyssac
Vézac, France
Château built at the end of the seventeenth century by Bernard Vernet for Bertrand de Marqueyssac, a
counselor of King Louis XIV. Under a new owner, Julien de Cerval, complete renovation of the garden in 1861.
Increasing neglect of the garden in the twentieth century. After systematic renovation by the new owner, Kleber
Rossillon, garden has been accessible to the public since 1996. Today there are more than 150,000 pruned
boxwood plants, as well as cypresses and linden trees on the grounds.

Central Garden at the Getty Center
Los Angeles, California
Architectural design by Peter Eisenman. Garden constructed in 1992, according to designs by Robert Irwin. Conceived as a total work of art for eyes, ears, and nose with the motto: "Always changing, never twice the same."
Left: Floating maze of azaleas.
Below: Bowls of plants on one of the stairways

Above top and right: The High Line
New York, New York
Railway line constructed in 1847 to supply the Meatpacking District. After numerous accidents, was elevated in 1929 as part of a city renovation project. Line discontinued in Fall 1980. From 1999, during Mayor Michael Bloomberg's administration, transformed into a park by Elizabeth Diller and Ricardo Scofidio.

Left: Broderie parterre *in the flower garden (Květná zahrada)*
Kroměříž, Czech Republic
Laid out in 1665–1675 by Filiberto Lucchese and Giovanni Pietro
Tencalla for Bishop Karl II von Liechtenstein-Kastelkorn

Left middle: A carpet of fallen blossoms in the gardens of Prague Castle
Prague, Czech Republic

Left below: Broderie parterre *of the Botanical Garden*
Brussels, Belgium
Laid out at the beginning of the twentieth century

Below: Boxwood spiral with a conically shaped tree in the
Vrtbovská Garden
Prague-Mala Strana, Czech Republic
Garden originally laid out in 1715–1720

Opposite: French broderie parterre *in the Jardim do Casa de Mateus*
Vila Real, Portugal
Original garden from the second half of the eighteenth century.
Redesigned in the 1930s/1940s. Decisive alterations later in the
twentieth century.

The trellises of the Lichte Allée (Bright Avenue) and arcades in the park of
the Schönbrunn Palace during the changing seasons
Vienna-Hietzing, Austria
The first gardens laid out in 1695 by Jean Trehet

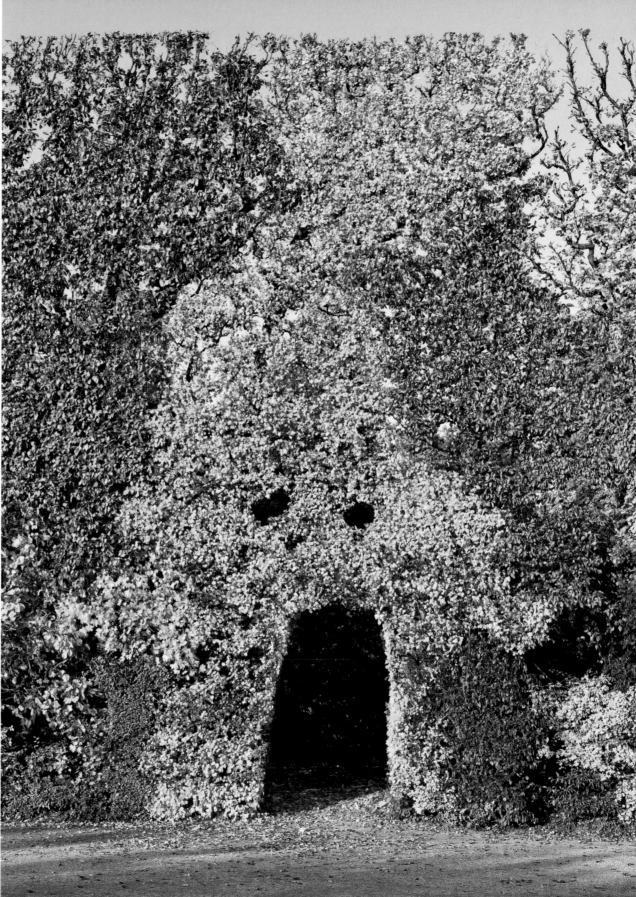

Opposite: Facade covered with three-pointed creeper (Parthenocissus Tricuspidata)
Aschach on the Danube, Austria
Expansion of the castle in 1606 under the Jörger family. From 1622, property of the
Harrach family.

Below: Facade of the Villa Balbiano covered with climbing fig (Ficus repens)
Lenno on Lake Como, Italy

Right: Facade of the former stable wing of the Gartenpalais Liechtenstein, covered in three-
pointed creeper. In the niche, a statue of Flora, first quarter of the eighteenth century.
Vienna-Rossau, Austria

ROOMS WITH SKY

The Courtyard Garden

As thesis and antithesis, there are two basic types of houses: the courtyard house, the layout of which revolves around a free space (courtyard), and the freestanding house that is surrounded by greenery.

Archaeological findings in China, Asia Minor, and Egypt provided us with evidence of the courtyard house, which has thus been documented from the beginning of human civilization. In many examples, mostly as burial objects, even three-dimensional models have been preserved that show prototypes of the courtyard house. The classical peristyle house of Greece and the Hellenistic world is a highly developed late form in which beautiful gardens could be created. The atrium house, which derived from the Greek source, defined the urban building culture of Roman antiquity, as well as the architecture of rural villas. In the course of the excavations of the villa sites—with their magnificent frescoes in Pompeii, Herculaneum, and the surrounding smaller settlements (Boscoreale, Boscotrecase, and Oplontis)—gardens were discovered that were preserved in remarkable condition, perfectly conserved by the lava or ash layers from the volcanic eruption of August 24, 79 A.D.—with sculptures and other decorations, and even furniture—conveying to us a vivid image of this culture.

Another tradition stems from the Islamic world, which in part was tightly connected to the culture of classical antiquity. This type of courtyard house is still present today in Persia and across the Middle East, all the way to the outermost northwest of Africa. In Syria's old towns of Aleppo and Damaskus, wonderful examples from the time of the Ottoman period (1517–1832 and 1840–1918) have been preserved. In Morocco's royal cities—in Fez, Marrakech, Meknes, and Rabat—courtyard houses, from small and humble versions to extremely luxurious ones that are still being constructed there today, characterize the urban fabric. Via Spain, this type even managed to reach Europe, where opulent examples of the Islamic courtyard house, such as the palaces in Granada, the Alhambra and the Generalife from the Nasrid Dynasty (1232–1492), are still standing—not least because of the preservation and reconstruction efforts already exerted in the nineteenth century. As in the basic Persian forms, the courtyards are either traversed by water canals (Alhambra, Myrthenhof, Generalife), which nourish the lush vegetation, or divided into four quadrants at the center by two crossing water canals, as is the case in the Court of the Lions with the famous Fountain of Lions at the Alhambra.

In the development of western architecture, the courtyards of abbeys and monasteries are the equivalent of examples from the East. Already sketched out in the plan of the monastery of Saint Gall (ca. 819–836), these abbeys had a whole sequence of courtyards that were assigned specific functions. The so-called *paradises* were situated in front of the church entrances, and the most important courtyard was always the cloister courtyard, which, as a general rule, was set up on the south side of the church. The cloister courtyards received the architecturally most sophisticated decor, with fountains and plants.

However, many very early examples were also preserved with courtyards that did not display green vegetation and were entirely paved instead. Here, representing a historical tradition lasting to this day, potted plants add the floral element to these "gardens" dominated by extreme architectural austerity. The major courtyard in the Abbazia di Praglia, one of the prominent Italian Benedictine abbeys,
is still described as a *chiostro botanico*. It represents a contrast to the courtyard called a *giardino pensile*, which is situated one story higher and serves as a water collector for the other lower-lying courtyards.

The monumental cloister courtyard of the Escorial in Madrid from the sixteenth century has a classical structure. Almost like a palace garden, it was created with a monumental fountain in the center. Entirely in contrast to this park, designed in an architecturally sophisticated manner, is the vastness of the large courtyard of the Certosa di Pavia in Italy, around which the twenty-three cells of the Carthusian monks who originally resided in the monastery are grouped (nowadays, Cistercians live there). The cloister courtyard of the Basilica of Saint Anthony of Padua—known as Il Santo—is also monumentally appointed. In 1810, a *Magnolia grandiflora* was planted there, which grew to enormous proportions and dominates the courtyard today.

Beginning in the eighteenth century and continuing into the nineteenth, trees increasingly became the characteristic design element of such courtyards in monasteries as well as palaces. Trees were used as green elements and providers of shade, and they formed a central oasis of calm; in most cases with a fountain. In the Cistercian monastery Heiligenkreuz (Holy Cross), south of Vienna, mighty plane trees—the ultimate fashionable tree at the turn of the nineteenth century—are standing in the Innerer Stiftshof (Inner Courtyard), which is located in front of the medieval core of the church and the monastery. There, together with the Dreifaltigkeitssäule (Holy Trinity Column; 1736–1739) and Josefsbrunnen (Joseph Fountain; 1739), by Giovanni Giuliani (1664–1744), they form a haven of tranquillity in the monastery, which has maintained its vitality and liveliness to this day. This courtyard, with the imperial wing laid in front of the actual monastery like a filter shielding it from the world. The situation was very similar at Tillysburg castle, close to St. Florian in Upper Austria. Here, as well, enormous trees marked a "room" that invited the visitor to pause and relax in the large courtyard, which was otherwise mercilessly exposed to the sun. The architectural features were more modest in the courtyard designs of the Beguines monasteries in Belgium and Holland, where the structures followed the happenstance of the city's layout, and open meadows are interspersed with trees.

In this spirit, gardens were created and trees were planted in the courtyards of many European cities. Here, the division between seclusion from the outer world and interior openness is never as extreme as it is in Arabic countries. During the eighteenth and nineteenth centuries, for example, there was a return to the type of house, mostly in Italy, where lavish green courtyards, planted with valuable trees, were created that informed the quality of urban life. As narrow, dark, uninviting, and forbidding as the streets of particularly northern Italian cities often seemed, when entering one of these patrician houses or palaces, one experienced another world that drew fresh air from its courtyards.

Chiostro del Capitolo o della Magnolia del Santo (Cloister of the Chapter or of the Saint's Magnolia)
Padua, Italy
Built in 1240. Alterations in the sixteenth century. The southern magnolia tree that dominates the courtyard was planted in 1810.

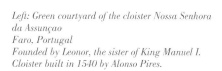

Left: Green courtyard of the cloister Nossa Senhora da Assunçao
Faro, Portugal
Founded by Leonor, the sister of King Manuel I.
Cloister built in 1540 by Alonso Pires.

Right above: Cloister walk (Claustro Real) of the Dominican cloister
Batalha, Portugal
Built between the fourteenth and sixteenth centuries by Alfonso Domingues and Master "Huguet" under the Portuguese kings Dom João I, Dom Duarte I, Dom Alfonso V, Dom João II, and Dom Manuel I

Right middle: Stone courtyard of the original castle of the Knights Templar
Tomar, Portugal
Cloister founded in 1160 by the Knights Templar. After the dissolution of the order by Pope Clemens V, from 1318, a cloister of the Order of the Knights of Christ, founded by King Denis. Great cloister walk built ca. 1550 under the influence of Palladianism by Diego de Torralva and Filippo Terzi for King Dom João II.

Right below: Great cloister walk of the Cistercian cloister
Alcobaça, Portugal
Cloister endowed in 1153 by King Dom Alonso I. The great cloister walk built in 1308 under King Denis.

The urban green oases of the Beguinages, originally homes of the Beguines
Bruges, Belgium

Right: Royal Beguinage Ten Wijngaarde (The Vineyard)
Endowed ca. 1230 by Johanna of Constantinople, Countess of Flanders. From 1299 under royal administration. The present-day houses built in the seventeenth century. After the death of the last Beguine, since 1930 the houses have been inhabited by Benedictine nuns.

Below: Beguinage Godshuis de Meulenaere, 1613
During the restoration of 1995, garden redesigned according to historical models

Opposite: The Great Courtyard of the Certosa (Charter House)
Certosa di Pavia, Italy
Founded in 1390 by Gian Galeazzo Visconti, Duke of Milan, as a Carthusian cloister. The cornerstone laid on August 27, 1396 by the architect Marco Scolari. Work was finished with the completion of the church facade in 1549. The cells of the twenty-three monks (today Cistercians) are located around the perimeter of the great cloister walk.

Left: The inner courtyard with the Holy Trinity Column and the Saint Joseph Fountain
Heiligenkreuz Abbey, Austria
Abbey founded in 1135/36 by Margrave Leopold III of Babenberg. The abbey's inner courtyard built from 1660. The Holy Trinity Column, 1736–1739, and Saint Joseph Fountain, 1739, created by Giovanni Giuliani.

Right and below: Tillysburg (Castle Tilly) courtyard
Saint Florian, Austria
Rebuilt in 1633 by Field Marshal Werner Tserklaes von Tilly. Staircase installed by Jakob Prandtauer for the later owner, the Abbey of Saint Florian.

Left: Courtyard of an urban palace with palm trees
Rovereto, Italy

Left below: Courtyard of the Palazzo Trivulzio
Milan, Italy
Original ensemble built in the sixteenth century.
Entire complex thoroughly renovated in 1707–1713.

Right: Courtyard of the Palazzo Borromeo-d'Adda
Milan, Italy
Modernized at the end of the eighteenth century by
Gerolamo Arganini

Garden of the Peter Paul Rubens town house
Antwerp, Belgium
Acquired in 1610 by Peter Paul Rubens and his wife, Isabella
Brant, two years after his return from Italy. Renovated, adding an
art room, an atelier, a colonnade, and a garden in the Italian style.
Garden re-created at the end of the twentieth century.

The tropical gardens of the Raffles Hotel
Singapore
Founded in 1887 by Armenian immigrants. Present building opened in 1899. Made famous by the novels of
Joseph Conrad, Rudyard Kipling, and Somerset Maugham.

Gardens and courtyards of the Alhambra
Granada, Spain
The present-day complex was created by Caliph Yusuf I (1333–1353) and Caliph Mohammed V (1353–1391) of the Nasrid Dynasty. After the Reconquista, the complex passed into the possession of the Catholic rulers of Spain, King Ferdinand II of Aragon and Queen Isabella I of Castile. Later expansion through the palace construction of Emperor Charles V. Afterward, slow deterioration of the Nasrid complex until it was rediscovered in the nineteenth century. Restoration and rebuilding from 1828.

Left above: Palacio de Partal Torre de las Damas

Left middle: The iron-gated courtyard (Reja Courtyard) with passageways between the Comares Tower and the chambers of Emperor Charles V

Left below: The Court of Machuca with small orange trees on the esplanade in front of the palaces of the Alhambra

Right: The Myrtle Patio

Gardens of the Generalife
Granada, Spain
*The palace and gardens of the Generalife constructed during
the reign of Caliph Mohammed III (1302–1309) and remodeled
shortly afterward by one of his successors, Caliph Abu I Walid
Isma'il (1313–1324). The complex is grouped around several
courtyards that are reminiscent of Persian architecture.*

Views of the green courtyards of town houses
Obidos, Portugal
The culture of Islamic houses with inner courtyards lives on in the intimate courtyards of Spanish and Portuguese cities.

Garden courtyards as a synthesis of Eastern and Western traditions
Venice, Italy

Left: Small front garden on the Canale Grande, opposite the Accademia

Right: Green courtyard on the Fondamento del Gafaro

Below: Green courtyard in front of the Church of San Giorgio dei Greci

Opposite: Courtyard of the Fondazione Querini Stampalia. The collection of Count Giovanni Querini Stampalia was donated to the city of Venice in 1868. Redesign of the ground floor and garden in 1961–1963 by Carlo Scarpa.

EVERYDAY OASES

The Small Garden

At an altitude of 5,850 feet, even a small garden would be rather unexpected. Yet high over the Valle di Gressoney, with a view of the Monte Rosa, is the tiny Walser village of Alpenzu, one of the last remaining intact settlements in the Alps. It contains a diminutive church, a few farmhouses—some of them from the seventeenth century—and a small vegetable garden that is quite surprising. The garden is carefully laid out, surrounded by a wall, and closed off by a wooden gate. The beds are separated by step plates, and between them the tiny lettuce plants strive to fulfill their destiny under the warm sun of high summer. This small piece of land, divided off from the rest of the earth and cultivated, calls to mind the strict order that reigns in cloister gardens, Renaissance gardens, or other gardens in the classical tradition.

This is just one of the many forms of small private gardens found surrounding farmhouses throughout Europe. The garden will lie a small distance from the courtyard, in the place best suited for growing, and will produce all the herbs and vegetables that a peasant family needs. It will be surrounded by a wall or by a little fence. The interior will perhaps be divided and framed by boxwoods, so that here, as in the world of the great gardens, the useful can be combined with the beautiful in a pleasing and beneficial way.

Rules do not apply in the private world of gardens. Still, it cannot be denied that there are certain regional and national preferences. The gardens of the Dutch castles and stately homes on the Vecht River between Utrecht and Muiden are very impressive. We recognize in their parterres, hedges, sculptures, vases, teahouses, and luxuriant ranks of plants the direct models for later domestic gardens. The richness experienced here influenced the rest of the country and appears again and again in the front gardens of bourgeois homes and farmhouses. The splendor of hydrangeas is seldom seen in such profusion as along the Vecht River or in Zaandijk and Zaanse Schans. Some of these lovely Baroque or neoclassical bourgeois residences and farmhouses still occupy their original locations, while others may be seen in open-air museums. The type of front-garden culture that once dominated large areas of the Central European domestic landscape is preserved here. The option of living on the ground floor was first made possible by front gardens that lent privacy and protection to a house. The loss of such front gardens certainly contributed to the triumph of the freestanding "villa" in a housing development since the original types of houses had to give way under the pressure of the expansion of road networks. The alternative—an aesthetically uninteresting little house surrounded on all sides by a bit of unformed space—is truly no substitute for the historic dwellings where the presence of a front garden and courtyard offered a nuanced series of free spaces.

Even in cities, the protective function of a small front garden has long been appreciated. The Hansa cities of northern Germany often make a very "green" impression because, in the absence of a thoroughly planned front garden, a small tree, a climbing rose, or a Virginia creeper is given the chance to spread up and across the facade of a house. Small front gardens create a certain distance from the hubbub of the streets for the row houses of London. An essential component of the quality of life in London would be lost if the blocks of the affluent residential areas of the city were deprived of their front gardens. There is also a finely differentiated hierarchy between fenced-in parks accessible only to residents with keys and the aforementioned front gardens or tiny backyard gardens.

It is no surprise that the idea of such garden types was imported to America. In the old cities of the New World, such as Boston, the appearance of front gardens characterizes entire neighborhoods. It is perhaps more amazing that such wonderful habitats exist even in the midst of the Upper East Side of Manhattan in New York City. In the streets of the city's Carnegie Hill district, sandstone facades covered entirely in green plants lend a certain airiness to entire blocks. The memory of the early settlement of America is evoked by the Colonial style of the oldest city houses, with their white-painted, flower-covered verandas. Sidewalk plantings, trees, and front gardens also establish a subtle buffer between the bustle of the street and domestic quiet. There is also a sort of urban architectural order that leads from the public space of the street through the semipublic front garden area to the privacy of residential life.

The holm oaks of Lucca in Italy contribute a rather curious aspect to the theme of the small garden. These trees are planted high up on the Torre Guinigi, a tower erected during the fourteenth century in the Via Sant'Andrea, directly in the middle of the urban fabric of Lucca. The tower was once one of more than 250 medieval towers built in the city for the protection of noble families. As at San Gimignano in Tuscany, these fortified towers once dominated the appearance of Lucca. Today a small garden and its five ancient holm oaks, planted as symbols of rebirth, sits atop the Torre Guinigi. The garden offers a panoramic view that extends over the entire city, all the way to the Mediterranean Sea.

The hanging gardens of the Trump Tower on Fifth Avenue in New York City is a similar oddity. They are perhaps somewhat disconcerting, but do represent a successful attempt to directly relate nature and human handiwork, tree and architecture. This is the latest of countless such attempts going back to the renowned Hanging Gardens of Semiramis in Babylon.

Recent decades have brought innovation in the form of such creations as Patrick Blanc's Vertical Garden. Blanc, a French botanist and artist, succeeded in spreading green in front of and onto facades in ways never before imagined. Such green facades are actually nothing new. What is new, however, is the sheer variety of plants that proliferates, as if in a garden, and covers the facade with a carpet of blossoms or variegated foliage. The theme of the front garden is reduced to a very small area that, however, combines architecture and garden in a new and unheard-of intensity. Blanc has set exciting new standards with his projects for the CaixaForum (Herzog & de Meuron, 2001–2007) in Madrid, the green wall on the Quai Branly Museum (Jean Nouvel, 2006), and the Sofitel Vienna Stephansdom hotel (Jean Nouvel, 2010).

Traversing balconies of the Majolikahaus
Vienna, Austria
Constructed in 1898/99 by architect Otto Wagner. Floral
facade decoration with majolica tiles, according to designs by
Alois Ludwig.

Garden of the Casa del Canova
Possagno, Italy
Antonio Canova was born in this house on November 1, 1757. At the suggestion of his brother, Giovanni Battista Sartori Canova, a Roman Catholic priest, a memorial to the most important sculptor of neoclassicism was constructed there. In 1826, four years after the death of the master, his atelier in Rome was closed and its contents transferred to Possagno. In 1834 the construction of a copy of the Roman atelier was begun, according to plans by Francesco Lazzari. The work was completed in 1836. The objects were placed on display in 1844. Bombardment by the Austrians inflicted heavy damage during World War I. In 1957, masterful structural extension by Carlo Scarpa.

Below left and left: The last rose in the garden of the house where Canova was born, with the monumental antique fragment of a foot clad in a sandal

Below right: Gouache by Antonio Canova

Left and right: Berrington Hall
Ludlow, England
Built at the beginning of the twentieth century

Below: Garden with pruned boxwoods from a town house on the
Contrescarpe
Bremen, Germany
Built at the end of the twentieth century

Left: Garden bench
Dunbar, Scotland

Right: Garden pavilion of a Baroque town house
Zurich, Switzerland

Below: The picturesque Villa Gaeta in its spacious garden on Lake Como
San Siro, Italy
Built in the 1920s by the architects Gino and Adolfo Coppedè for the industrialist family
Ambrosoli of Milan. Filming location for the final scene of the 2006 James Bond film
Casino Royale.

Left: Historical boundary wall of the
Gartenpalais Liechtenstein
Vienna-Rossau, Austria

Right: Small vegetable garden in the Walser
village Alpenzu, 5,850 feet above sea level
Alpenzu, Italy

Below: Garden fence painted in green and white
Zaanse Schans, the Netherlands

*Typical Dutch houses with painted wood and brick facades and lush
front gardens planted with hydrangeas
Zaanse Schans (below and left) and Zaandijk (right)*

Town houses with front gardens
New York, New York
Early nineteenth century

Torre Guinigi with holm oaks
Lucca, Italy
Tower constructed in the fourteenth century

The Hanging Gardens of the Trump Tower
New York, New York
Constructed for Donald Trump, according to designs by Der Scutt of Swanke, Hayden &
Connell Architects. Completed on November 30, 1983.

DIALOGUES BETWEEN
TRADITION AND INNOVATION

The New Garden

The history of the garden has entered a completely new territory in modern times. It is not so much formal or aesthetic conditions that have changed but rather the realities of function. Alongside the existing garden types and activities, new goals have arisen that derive from the transitions and upheavals of the mid-nineteenth century.

One essential development was the process of "defortification" that took place in Europe, beginning slowly and then accelerating rapidly. Through this process cities gained a great potential for development and new free space to be reconceptualized and utilized. To some extent this affected the medieval fortifications of many cities, whose inhabitants transformed the walls in various ways into green spaces rather than tearing them down. The free spaces on the outskirts of towns were used by the adjacent residences to establish an enchanting landscape of small gardens. A number of cities in northern Italy were able to preserve their medieval fortifications as municipal recreation areas. It is very impressive to walk along the walls of the fortress of Montagnana in a complete circumnavigation of the city. The circuit of the bastions of Lucca in Tuscany is perhaps an even more intense experience. From one side of the walls, one looks down into the thickly woven maze of the medieval metropolis; from the other side, across broad unspoiled meadows and fields.

A similar interim solution was attempted in Vienna. A mighty ring of bastions encircled the inner city; in front of them lay the *glacis*, an open green space, and beyond the *glacis*, the outer districts of the town. In the nineteenth century a wonderful small garden, the present-day Volksgarten (People's Garden), was laid out in close proximity to the imperial Hofburg Palace. A famous coffeehouse, the Cortische Kaffeehaus, opened in the park. The Theseion, a temple of Theseus, was built by Pietro Nobile (1774–1854) between 1819 and 1823 as a monument to the defeat of Napoleon Bonaparte's France. A Theseus sculptural group that had originally been commissioned by Bonaparte was displayed in the temple, and in its cellar the antiquities collection of the Austrian imperial house was exhibited. Long after the destruction of the city fortifications and the construction of the Ringstrasse, with its splendid representative buildings, the Volksgarten is still a beloved inner-city recreation area.

In the course of this reorientation, parks and ornamental squares were laid out in many parts of Vienna and became characteristic of the urban panorama of the *Gründerzeit*, the later nineteenth century. The Viennese Stadtpark was created in the old style by the landscape painter Joseph Selleny (1824–1875), with modifications in 1861 by the city gardener Rudolf Siebeck (1812–1878). A very important attraction was added between 1903 and 1907 during the course of the regulation of the Wienfluss: an effluent of the Danube Canal. The architect Friedrich Ohmann (1858–1927) and the more progressive Josef Hackhofer (1863–1917) together created a park in the art nouveau style at the spot where the stream enters the Stadtpark. The ensemble includes pavilions, sculptures, monumental ceramic amphorae, walls and beds of plants, ponds, staircases, balustrades, and benches. The park was originally enclosed by a heavy cast-iron fence. Until 1956 visitors had to pay a fee to the "*Sesselweiber*"—female seat guardians—if they wanted to sit in one of the cast-iron seats placed around the park.

One of the most beautiful examples of an urban ornamental space is the park on the Friedrichsplatz in Mannheim that surrounds the historic water tower built from 1886 to 1889, according to plans of Gustav Halmhuber (1862–1936). From about 1899 to 1903, the Berlin architect Bruno Schmitz (1858–1916) meticulously constructed

in the park a green space furnished with a monumental pergola and a cascade. Along with the city's Baroque castle and garden, this park is Mannheim's second trademark. The parks of the nobility were frequently turned into grounds open to the larger public. Typical of this is the Parque del Buen Retiro (Park of the Pleasant Retreat) in Madrid, laid out in 1632 by Alonso Carbonell (1583–1660) for King Philip IV of Spain (1605–1665). After its destruction during the Napoleonic Wars, the garden was gradually made accessible to the public. Parts of the garden were even redesigned and newly laid out during the past decade. On the shore of an artificial lake in the center of the park stands the monument to King Alfonso XII of Spain (1857–1885). The Palacio de Cristal (Crystal Palace), built in 1887 as a tropical greenhouse and now used as an exhibition center, is also in the Parque del Buen Retiro.

The most important of these municipal green spaces is, without a doubt, Central Park in New York City, an artificial creation begun in 1859 as the "green heart" of the metropolis. What today appears as a piece of nature preserved from the building craze that enveloped New York was actually constructed on a part of the city that had seriously deteriorated. The houses on the land had to be laboriously razed before it could return to a relatively natural condition. The 1,600 inhabitants of the area were evicted under the rule of eminent domain in 1857 and work began. The park was constructed in accordance to the plans of Frederick Law Olmsted (1822–1903) and Calvert Vaux (1824–1895), the winners of the Central Park Commission's landscape design contest. By 1869 more than 20,000 workers had been employed on the project. In the middle of the park lies a large expanse of water, the Jacqueline Kennedy Onassis Reservoir. There is only one other large building in the park, the Metropolitan Museum of Art, which in the first phase of its construction opened on February 20, 1872.

One of the favorite activities of city planners is making urban spaces more attractive by designing new parks. A good example of this is the "reconquest" of the High Line in New York City. Originally built as a railway line into the Meatpacking District, it soon became obsolete and lay unused for many years. As this neighborhood in Manhattan became a more desirable living area, a new use was sought for the neglected railway line. The search for a new purpose was supported by the citizens of the community (Friends of the High Line), and in 1999 the transformation into an elevated, artificially created park was undertaken. The first part of the railway park opened in 2009 and the second in 2011. The planning and realization of the High Line Park was the responsibility of the landscape architect James Corner (b. 1961) of James Corner Field Operations, the Dutch garden designer Piet Oudolf (b. 1944), and the architectural design studio Diller Scofidio + Renfro.

The attempt to achieve positive urban development by building new parks is paralleled by the construction of spectacular new museum and performing arts buildings in the past few years. In the case of the Millennium Park in Chicago, the initiative for installing the Lakefront Gardens for the Performing Arts in the disused Randolph Street Terminals of the Illinois Central Railroad came from various organizations. The idea originated in 1977 but was only realized beginning in 1997, when the City of Chicago mandated that a hall for musical events be built there. The architect Frank Gehry (b. 1929) received the commission and built the Jay Pritzker Pavilion as the focal point of the Millennium Park. The pavilion possesses a huge stage and a thrilling roof space. It crowns a park where architecture, sculpture, and landscape are integrated in an exemplary manner and redefine the relationship between the city and the shore of Lake Michigan. The spectacular expansion of the neighboring Art Institute of Chicago building, the Modern Wing, designed by Renzo Piano (b. 1937), opened in 2009. Contemporary art was incorporated into the project itself. One can look from the roof of the museum, over the Nichols Bridgeway—also erected by Piano—into the grounds of the park. The park's exciting structures, sculptures, and plants help to unify landscape and architecture. In Milwaukee, the Spanish architect and engineer Santiago Calatrava (b. 1951) accomplished a similar feat by more closely connecting the city with the shore of Lake Michigan by means of his spectacular new Milwaukee Art Museum addition, the Quadracci Pavilion (2001). The Cudahy Gardens, built according to a design of Dan Kiley (1912–2004), surround the museum and are integrated into the total composition.

Museums and gardens have engaged in a completely new dialogue in recent decades. Closed-off and claustrophobic as museums can often seem, a liberating view from a window into open nature can hardly be surpassed by even the most beautiful painting. In this competition between art and nature, the latter is often victorious. Fountains and ponds in the open spaces beside a museum can project a vivid light that the most ingeniously produced artificial light cannot hope to match. Louis I. Kahn (1901–1974) demonstrated this old trick to the whole world at his Kimbell Art Museum in Fort Worth, Texas, built between 1966 and 1972. Just across the street, at the Modern Art Museum of Fort Worth, the Japanese architect Tadao Ando (b. 1941) used Kahn's principle by placing the individual pavilions in a large artificial pond. Piano also made use of this idea on a much smaller scale in his Fondation Beyeler (1991–1997) in Riehen, a town near Basel, Switzerland. Sculptures such as Giacometti's *Grande Femme III* and *L'Homme Qui Marche II*, both of 1960, surrounded by the shimmering movement of the pond, are very impressive.

Sculpture gardens created during the twentieth century may be regarded as worthy successors to the gardens and parks of the Baroque era, which were often filled with hundreds of sculptures. In the modern sculpture garden, architecture, art, and nature have once again coalesced into a unified whole, as was the case three hundred years ago. A good example of this is the Tuileries Garden in Paris. As a result of the fire that occurred during the uprising of the Paris Commune in 1871, and deterioration during the following decades, the Tuileries was largely destroyed. When the city decided to revitalize the gardens, the project fortunately included the installation of splendid bronze and lead sculptures on the grounds. Masters of modern sculpture were represented—Aristide Maillol, Henry Laurens, Henry Moore, Jean Dubuffet—and their works were supplemented by contemporary pieces of similar stature, resulting in an unequalled sculpture garden in the midst of metropolitan Paris.

Sculpture gardens have made possible an entirely new relationship between nature, architecture, and art. At the Fondation Marguerite et Aimé Maeght, in Saint-Paul-de-Vence, France, the close collaboration between the Maeghts and the Catalan architect Josep Lluís Sert (1902–1983) created a unique symbiosis of nature and human design. Almost fifty years after it was opened by André Malraux in 1964, it still draws hundreds of thousands of visitors every year. Masterpieces by Bonnard, Braque, Calder, Chagall, Cillida, Giacometti, Léger, and Miró carry on a dialogue with Sert's architecture and with the intoxicating light and fragrance of the Provençal landscape. The experience is just as intense at the Kröller-Müller Museum near Otterloo, the Netherlands. This museum was also founded by enthusiastic art collectors, the couple Helene Kröller-Müller and Anton Kröller, and given to the Netherlands in 1935. Finally, the Louisiana Museum of Modern Art near Copenhagen should be mentioned. It presents works of sculpture in a much more open way to visitors: on the shore of the Öresund straits. The museum, which today contains more than three thousand works of art, was created in 1958 as a private institution by Knud Jensen (1916–2000) and later became a foundation.

In the nineteenth century William Drummond of Scotland already conceived the Valley Cemetery in Stirling as more than just a last resting place for the dead. In 1863 he expanded the cemetery and renamed it Drummond's Pleasure Ground. While truly desiring to allow the dead their eternal rest under the sod, he also wanted to invite the living to experience the area as a park. In it he erected the Star Pyramid, a memorial to the heroes and martyrs of Presbyterianism. Soon afterward tours were already being conducted to the novel attraction. The Valley Cemetery is an extremely early example of the understanding of the cemetery as a garden and park, an idea that has been frequently discussed in the twentieth century.

With the design for the Skogskyrkogården (The Woodland Cemetery), in Stockholm, Sweden, in the early twentieth century, a park was created that could not be ignored by any architect active in this field. After winning a competition for the project in 1915, the victorious architects Erik Gunnar Asplund (1885–1940) and Sigurd Lewerentz (1885–1975) were given the commission for its planning and realization. The cemetery was not completed until 1940. The most magnificent aspect of the cemetery is its incredible spaciousness and emptiness. Visitors who walk through it are nevertheless given a sense of order and orientation by architectural features that are both carefully incorporated into the surroundings and precisely articulated. The effect recalls the dialogue between nature and art that fills the landscapes of the early German Romantic painter Caspar David Friedrich (1774–1840) with creative tension and draws viewers into their depths. Although a giant granite cross dominates the cemetery, it is still a place that respects the freedom of dissenters.

One of the mavericks of twentieth-century European architecture, Jože Plečnik (1872–1957), approached the subject from a very different direction. In his design for the cemetery of Zale in Ljubljana, Slovenia, Plečnik availed himself of the formal language and typology of antiquity when he built a small memorial chapel, where people were often laid out before burial, in the midst of more traditional holy ground. The rationality of northern Protestantism seen in the Skogskyrkogården was combined here with a Croatian Catholicism whose sources are deeply rooted in the traditions of antiquity. The Italian architect Carlo Scarpa (1906–1978) set the third milestone in the evolution of the last garden that we experience on this earth. Between 1970 and 1972 he carried out the expansion of the cemetery of San Vito di Altivole, a town south of Asolo in northern Italy, to accommodate the tomb of the Brions, a Venetian industrialist family. Although it is a Catholic cemetery, Scarpa did not incorporate the tradition of the surroundings but rather drew on his experience as a cosmopolitan architect. He was influenced by Asia and its gardens, and he used their qualities in a freely associative way. From the circular gate with its interlinked rings, providing a gentle reminiscence of the garden culture of China, we are led to a broad arch that resembles the heavens spread out in a medieval panel painting. Under this arch the coffins of the Brions, the benefactor couple, lean toward each other. In this last garden, through Carlo Scarpa, they have rediscovered the memory of paradise lost.

*Propylaea and memorial chapel in the cemetery
at Žale
Ljubljana, Slovenia
Built in 1938–1940 by Jože Plečnik*

Skogskyrkogården (The Woodland Cemetery) in an artificially created landscape (Gravel pit in the foreground) Stockholm-Enskede, Sweden
Built in 1917–1940 by Gunnar Asplund and Sigurd Lewerentz after winning an architectural competition in 1912

Left: Crematorium and Holy Cross Chapel with colonnaded hall and cross in front

Right: Gardeners' Building

Below: Meditation Grove crowned with elm trees. Inspired by the landscape paintings of Caspar David Friedrich.

Tomb of the Brion family
San Vito di Altivole, Italy
Built in 1970–1978 by Carlo Scarpa for
Onorina Brion Tomasin

*Pavilions and sculptures of the Fondation
Marguerite et Aimé Maeght
Saint-Paul-de-Vence, France
Built for Marguerite and Aimé Maeght by the
Catalan architect Josep Lluís Sert, in close
collaboration with artists such as Miró,
Chagall, Braque, and Giacometti. Opened on
July 24, 1964.*

Modern Art Museum of Fort Worth
Fort Worth, Texas
Built in 2002 by Tadao Ando

Left and below: View of the museum pavilions. Left, the sculpture
Conjoined *by Roxy Paine, 2007.*
Right: Vortex by Richard Serra, 2002

Kimbell Art Museum
Fort Worth, Texas
Built by Louis I. Kahn for the board of directors of the Kimbell Art Foundation. Opened 1972.
Intensive integration of interior and exterior spaces; optimal use of natural light by reflection from large water surfaces.

Right above: View of the courtyard of the restaurant, with Aristide Maillol's L'Air (model, 1938; casting, 1962)

Right middle: Figure in a Shelter by Henry Moore, 1983

Below: View of the courtyard that opens to the sculpture garden on the west side of the museum

Far right: View of the west side of the museum with Fernand Léger's La fleur qui marche (Running Flower), 1952

Fondation Beyeler
Basel-Riehen, Switzerland
Built in 1994–1997 by Renzo Piano on the grounds of the
Villa Berower for Ernst Beyeler

Below: View of the sculpture garden with Alexander Calder's
The Tree, *1996, and Ellsworth Kelly's* White Curve, *2001*
*Bottom and right: View of the northeast and southwest ends of
the museum*

Left and below: The Art Institute of Chicago, Modern Wing, Museum Courtyard
Chicago, Illinois
Built by Renzo Piano and completed in 2009. The revitalization of the shore area
on Lake Michigan by the redesign of the Millennium Park includes the expansion
of the Art Institute of Chicago, the Jay Pritzker Pavilion by Frank Gehry, and the
contributions of numerous artists.

Above: Chicago Millennium Park, Cloud Gate
Chicago, Illinois
Built in 2004–2006 by Anish Kapoor

The gardens of the Quai Branly Museum
Paris, France
Architecture by Jean Nouvel. Garden
architecture by Gilles Clément. Vertical garden
of the administrative building by Patrick
Blanc. Opened in 2006.

Sculpture garden of the Kröller-Müller Museum
Otterloo, the Netherlands
Founded by Helene Kröller-Müller and Anton Kröller. First important acquisition in 1909. Collection donated to the state and accessible to the public since 1935. Sculpture garden opened in 1961.
Left: Amphitheater by Marta Pan, 2007. Design, 2005.
Below: Squares with Two Cities by Barbara Hepworth, 1963–1964, in front of the pavilion by Gerrit Rietfeld, 1964–1965. Design, 1954/55.
Opposite: K-Piece by Mark Di Suvero, 1973

Opposite: Sculpture garden of the Kröller-Müller Museum
Otterloo, the Netherlands
Rocky Lumps *by Tom Claassen, 2005–2006. Design, 2004.*

Parco Basso (Sculpture Park) of Venaria Reale
Venaria Reale, Italy
Built by Filippo Juvara and Benedetto Alfieri, ca. 1730. Castle renovated in 1998. The re-creation of the lost Baroque garden is in progress. New interpretation by the Italian minimalist Giuseppe Penone, using fourteen monumental installations.
Right: Tra scorza e scorza (Between Bark and Bark) *by Giuseppe Penone, 2003–2007*
Below: Verso la luce (Toward the Light) *by Giuseppe Penone, 2003–2007*

Jardin des Tuileries
Paris, France
Original garden laid out in 1564
for Caterina de' Medici. Remodeled
by André Le Nôtre for King Louis
XIV. Ravaged during the French
Revolution. Restoration after 1981
under François Mitterand.

Left: Méditerranée *by Aristide*
Maillol, 1905

Right: Le Bel Costumé *by*
Jean Dubuffet, 1973

Below: Rivière *by Aristide Maillol,*
1943

President's Gardens of the Prague Castle
Prague, Czech Republic
Constructed in 1920–1935 by Josef Plečnik

Left above: View from the Garden on the Ramparts (1923–1926) past the Obelisk to the Church of Saint Nicholas in the Old City

Left below and below: Lookout point with view of the Hirschgraben

Right: Paradise Garden with the large granite basin. In the background, Prague Castle.

Left, below, and opposite left: Friedrichsplatz with the Water Tower
Mannheim, Germany
The square constructed in 1899–1903, according to plans by the Berlin architect
Bruno Schmitz. The Water Tower, erected in 1886–1889 as a monumental brick
construction, according to plans by the Stuttgart architect Gustav Halmhuber.
The construction of the Water Tower was the result of an architectural
competition held in 1885. The full ensemble is considered one of the most
beautiful examples of urban ornamental squares created in the second half of the
nineteenth century and the early twentieth century.

Right: Cast-iron flower basin in Central Park
New York, New York

Central Park
New York, New York
Based on the ideas and preliminary plans by Andrew Jackson Downing. Construction of the landscaped park began in 1859 and followed the designs submitted by Frederick Law Olmsted and Calvert Vaux, winners of the project competition. Park completed in 1873. Before the project could be realized, 1,600 inhabitants of the area had to be evicted, and a vast amount of earth was transported from New Jersey in order to make the inhospitable terrain suitable for the growth of plants.

Left above: View from the roof of the Metropolitan Museum of Art toward Midtown Manhattan

Left middle and below: There are signs everywhere of how difficult it was to carve the park out of nature

Right: View over the large Jacqueline Kennedy Onassis Reservoir toward the West Side

428

INDEX

Page numbers in italics refer to captions.

Additional Photos

Jacket front: Villa Torrigiani di Camigliano,
  Camigliano-Lucca, Italy
Jacket back: Monticello, Charlottesville, Virginia
Page 4: Vrtbovská zahrada (Vrta Garden), Prague,
  Czech Republic
Page 6: Gardens of the Lion Grove (Shizi Lin),
  Suzhou, People's Republic of China
Page 13: Villa Lante, Bagnaia, Italy
Page 79: Château de Versailles, Versailles, France
Page 117: Yuyuan Garden, Shanghai, People's
  Republic of China
Page: 147: Korin-in-Temple, Kyoto, Japan
Page 195: Josef Rebell, *Wooded Landscape with
  Temple*, oil on canvas, 1809
Page 259: Désert de Retz, Chambourcy, France
Page 299: Palm House in the park at Schönbrunn
  Palace, Vienna-Hietzing, Austria
Page 319: Palais Het Loo, Apeldoorn, the
  Netherlands
Page 335: Villa del Balbianello, Lenno on Lake
  Como, Italy
Page 357: Cloister walk (Claustro Real) of the
  Dominican cloister, Batalha, Portugal
Page 381: Garden in the House of Francesco
  Petrarch, Arqua, Italy
Page 399: Skogskyrkogården (The Woodland
  Cemetery), Stockholm, Sweden

Photo Credits

29 right, Galleria Carlo Virgilio, Arte Moderna e
Contemporanea, Rome; 56, Kupfälzisches Museum
der Stadt Heidelberg, Heidelberg, Germany; 57
below, 90 left, 199 above and below, 262 right, 289
right, 295 right above, private collection, Vienna; 82
below, Grand Trianon, Versailles; 94, private collection, Bruck an der Leitha, Austria; 96 above, Öster-
reichische Nationalbibliothek, Vienna; 96 below,
MAK, Museum für angewandte Kunst, Vienna; 97,
141, 195, 200, 222, 223 above, 226, 227 above and
middle, 231 below, 243 left above and left below,
262 left, 276 below, 277, 289 left below, 292 left,
293 left, 294 below, 305 left above, 308 below, 310
right below, Liechtenstein. The Princely Collections,
Vienna; 127 below, Museum Rietberg, Zurich; 199
middle, 293 above middle, 294 above, Niederöster-
reichisches Landesarchiv, St. Pölten, Austria; 201,
224 above, 288, 289 left above and left middle,
Albertina, Vienna; 220, 221, Sammlung Esterhàzy,
Eisenstadt, Austria; 227 below, Belvedere, Vienna

All photographs by Johann Kräftner, represented by
Imagno Brandstätter Images, Vienna, except as
noted above.

© imagno.com

Würthgasse 14
A-1190 Vienna
Austria
www.imagno.com

Editor: Andreas Deppe and Astrid Göttche
Graphic Design: Johann Kräftner
Production: Clemens Hutter

First published in the United States of America in
2012 by
Rizzoli International Publications, Inc.
300 Park Avenue South
New York, NY 10010
www.rizzoliusa.com

Originally published in German in 2012 by
Christian Brandstätter Verlag
GmbH & Co KG
Wickenburggasse 26
A-1080 Vienna
www.cbv.at

© 2012 by Christian Brandstätter Verlag, Vienna

2012 2013 2014 2015 / 10 9 8 7 6 5 4 3 2 1

ISBN: 978-0-8478-3928-5

Library of Congress Control Number: 2012934943

Printed in China